THE LIFE OF SAINT TERESA

LOGOS-93

SAINT TERESA OF JESUS. (Anonymous. Real Academia de la Lengua, Madrid).

P. CRISÓGONO

THE LIFE
OF
SAINT TERESA

2.ª edición

EDITORIAL DE ESPIRITUALIDAD

Triana, 9 - 28016 MADRID

www.editorialdeespiritualidad.com

editorial@editorialdeespiritualidad.com

Cover design: Víctor M. Espinosa

Original Title:
VIDA DE SANTA TERESA

© by Editorial de Espiritualidad, Madrid

THE LIFE OF SAINT TERESA
English translation by Kevin Bruton

© by Editorial de Espiritualidad
   Madrid, 2011

ISBN: 978-84-7068-394-7
Depósito legal: M. 35.561-2011

Impreso en España – Printed in Spain

Fotocomposición e impresión: Closas-Orcoyen, S. L.
Polígono Igarsa. Paracuellos de Jarama (Madrid)

PROLOGUE

Ana of Saint Bartholomew, an exceptional wit-
ness of the death of Saint Teresa, testifies that when
the saint saw that they were going to bring her the
Viaticum, she exclaimed with great joy: «My Lord,
the time to journey has arrived». Teresa, who had
arrived at Alba de Tormes so worn down from de
journey that it seemed as though she didn't have a
healthy bone left in her body, died happily thinking
of setting out on a new journey.

This long awaited journey, out of time and with-
out fatigue, has been going on for four centuries,
and in our days it has experienced an acceleration,
only comparable with that which occurred in the
seventeenth century. That is why, with reason and
without clichés, we can talk about Teresian rele-
vance at all levels.

The proclamation of her as the first woman Doc-
tor of the Church and patroness of Spanish writers,
the translations of her works into all languages and
the uninterrupted editions of these translations, the
study of her works undergone by Catholics and non-
Catholics are all proofs of this evident relevance.

However, her most faithful public, today as well as during her life, has always been constituted by the most common and simple of people. These are the people for whom Fr. Crisógono has written this Life of Saint Teresa. *The success of Fr. Crisógono in doing this is evident, considering how quickly all the previous editions have been sold out, the last of which was twenty five thousand copies.*

We now offer this new edition in English, profusely illustrated, with the hope that the public will receive it with the same enthusiasm that has lead so many editions in Spanish to be sold out.

E. D. E.

Translator's Note

In the translation, we have tried to maintain the direct and colourful language that Fr. Crisógono used in the Spanish version. In this way we hope to offer to English readers the elegance of his literary ability that makes this Life of Saint Teresa, *not only a devout, but also a very entertaining reading experience.*

I believe I can say that the work to make this edition a reality has been done with the most sincere desire that the immense spiritual treasures found in the life and works of Saint Teresa may inspire evermore people to discover the great joy and plenitude found in the following of Christ.

Many thanks to Fr. Greg Homeming for his very much appreciated assistance in the translation.

Kevin Bruton, Pbro

TERESIAN CHRONOLOGY

1515   March 28: Teresa is Born. She is given the name Teresa de Cepeda y Ahumanda.

April 4: Teresa is baptized in the Parish of San Juan.

1516   Charles V ascends to the Spanish throne. Later he will be crowned Emperor.

1519   The Lutheran schism is consumated.

1523   Teresa, together with her brother Rodrigo, attempts to flee to the «Land of the Moors».

1531   Teresa enters the Augustinian convent of Santa Maria de Gracia in Avila as a boarding student.

Henry VIII breaks away from the Roman Church.

1535   November 2: Teresa flees from home and enters the Carmelite Monastery of the Encarnación.

1536   November 2: Teresa is clothed with the habit of a Carmelite Nun. She makes her profession on the same day of the following year.

1538   Teresa is forced to leave the monastery because of a mysterious illness, which makes her go to Becedas to be placed under the care of a woman healer.

1543   December 26: Don Alonso, Teresa's father, dies. He is assisted at his deathbed by Teresa.

1545   Innauguration of the Council of Trent.

1554   Lenten Season: Teresa's conversion before an Image of the Scourging of Our Lord.

1555   Charles V abdicates the Spanish Crown in favor of his son Philip II.

1560   Teresa receives the Mystical Grace of the Transfixion or the Grace of the Arrow. This same year she decides to found a reformed monastery.

1562   August 24: Innauguration of the Monasterio de San José de Ávila. This is Teresa's first foundation of nuns.

1563   Conclusion of the Council of Trent.

1565   Teresa finishes the second redaction of the *Book of Life*.

1566/67   August: Innauguration of the Foundation of Medina del Campo (of nuns) and first meeting with St. John of the Cross in the same town.

1568   Foundation of monasteries of nuns in Malagon and Valladolid.

            November 28: Innauguration of the Teresian reform of the male branch of the Order in Duruelo (Avila) with the collaboration of St. John of the Cross.

1569   Foundation of monasteries of nuns in Toledo and Pastrana (Guadalajara). The foundation of a convent for friars in Pastrana.

1570   Foundation of a monastery of nuns in Salamanca.

1571   Foundation of a monastery of nuns in Alba de Tormes (Salamanca). Teresa is appointed prioress of the Old Monastery of the Encarnacion in Avila.

1572   Teresa has St. John of the Cross appointed as confessor in the Monastery of the Incarnation in Avila. Upon receiving Holy Communion from his hands, Teresa receives the grace of Spiritual Matrimony on the 18th of November.

1574   Foundation of a monastery of nuns in Segovia. In October, she finishes her term as prioress of the Encarnacion in Avila.

1575   Foundation of monasteries of nuns in Beas de Segura (Jaen) and Seville.

1576   Foundation of a monastery of nuns in Caravaca de la Cruz (Murcia).

1577   In Toledo, Teresa begins writing the *Interior Castle*. She finishes writing it in Avila at the end of this year. On December, St. John of the Cross is taken prisoner in Avila and is transferred to Toledo.

1578   August: St. John of the Cross escapes from prison in Toledo.

1580   Foundation of monasteries of nuns in Villanueva de la Jara (Albacete) and Palencia.

1581   The Chapter of Separation of the Discalced Friars is held with the promulgation of the constitution of an autonomous province of Discalced Carmelite Friars in April. Foundation of a monastery of nuns in Soria. In November, Teresa and John of the Cross meet for the last time in Avila.

1582   Foundation of a monastery of nuns in Burgos. Teresa travels from Medina to Alba de Tormes, where she dies on the 4th of October at nine in the evening. She exclaims: *At last, I die as a daughter of the Church.*

1614   Teresa of Jesus is beatified by Pope Paul V.

1622   Teresa is canonized by Pope Gregory XV.

1970   Paul VI declares Saint Teresa of Jesus Doctor of the Church.

FAÇADE OF THE CHURCH OF THE SAINT. Engraving of the nineteenth century.

CHAPTER I

A NOBLE CASTILLIAN HOME

It's a cold morning on the 28th of March in the year 1515 in Avila. The sun hasn't risen yet. The city sleeps silently enclosed in its walls of granite, crowned by more than two thousand parapets. The streets are whitened by the snow and they still conserve, in the solitude of the night, a tranquillity of cloistered silence.

From some narrow and long windows, subtle rays of light, and noises of joyfulness stream out. It's one of the houses close to the southern wall: a house with walls of granite, and a small back garden. Above the door, there is a coat of arms engraved in stone, formed by stripes and circles,

FAÇADE OF THE CHURCH OF THE SAINT. Erected during the first third of the seventeenth century on the site in which the house of Mr. Alonso Sánchez de Cepeda had occupied and which, in that time, was found quite deteriorated and transformed.

crossed spades and rampant lions. It's the house of Mr. Alonso Sánchez de Cepeda and Mrs. Beatriz de Ahumada.

It has spacious rooms and a noble air. There are knight's spades and spurs, spears and crossbows, leather and small wooden shields, golden sashes and glittering war helmets. There are Dutch sheets, long shirts of gold, tunics from Valencia and coat of mail from Damasco, all stored in the chests. On the shelves, there can be seen books on history and literature, devotional books, lives of saints, the works of Cicero and of Seneca, poetry of Juan de Mena and Virgil, the Gospels... and on the table there are crosses shining with gold and silver chains, there are blest candles and a chess set with ivory figures.

Five children and some relatives move about in the rooms and corridors. The family is celebrating: a baby girl has born. Nobody noticed anything extraordinary about the birth. There hasn't been an apparition of stars over the house, nor any prophetical dreams announcing a glorious future for the baby. On the other hand, her presence seems to produce a strange sensation that nobody can explain: a kind of instinct that

CHAPEL OF BIRTH. This chapel occupies a part of what was the bedroom of the saint's parents and in which she was born on the 28th of March, 1515.

BAPTISMAL FONT. In this baptismal font, in Saint John's Parish Church, Teresa was baptised on the 4th of April, 1515.

impels you to look at that small angel of rosy flesh as a being of the highest of destinies.

* * *

A few days later, around the 4th of April, before the large and decorated entrance of the palace of Núñez Vela, very close to the house of Cepeda, there is a hustle of people and the rejoicing of children. From the windows that look towards the entrance of the city walls, there are some embroidered damasks hanging down with their silk flowers. The bells are pealing on St. John's Church and a group of people in their Sunday's best leave the palace and start making their way towards the parish church. On their left, they pass the Superunda Palace, they keep going, following a small and winding alley until they reach the portico of the church. Mr. Francisco Núñez Vela, dressed as a knight with cape and sword, and Mrs. María del Aguila, daughter of Governor of the city, are leading at the head of the group. They are carrying the daughter of Alonso Sánchez de Cepeda wrapt in white laced garments. They are going to christen her. Next to the baptismal font, in that wide open nave, the name of Teresa is heard for the first time.

When the joyful procession leaves the church, and heads back to the palace of Francisco Núñez, from the north, the soft sound of a convent bell is heard: the convent of the Incarnation is being inaugurated, the one that will be the future home of the recently baptised baby. Teresa will immortalise it. You could say that the small bell was already calling her, greeting her from the high bricked tower.

* * *

Seven years have past. An oil-lamp with three stemming flames is giving light to the room from the centre of the table. On one side, Mrs. Beatriz de Ahumada is sowing; Mr. Alonso is writing the accounts of the day; Teresa and her brother Rodrigo, while inclining their heads over the table, read out the engraved letters they see on the yellowed pages of a book. It's about the lives

CONVENT OF THE SAINT and on the right, the façade of Saint Scholastica's Hospital.

FAÇADE (detail) OF SAINT JOHN'S PARISH CHURCH. ▶

of saints. The first is an anchorite who lives in solitude many years and the only company he has are the wild animals who serve him. Then there is a virgin with a very innocent expression and a white vestment which makes her seemingly capable of moving almost without touching the ground. Then there is a martyr: a tyrant condemns him for confessing his faith in Christ; some executioners cut his head off at one go, and he flies straight to heaven, surrounded by angels, palms and crowns. Teresa's eyes glow with enthusiasm: "Glory forever and ever and ever". The children repeat this phrase, and are absorbed thinking about it, while their parents, taking note of this, look at each other in silence.

The next day neither Teresa nor Rodrigo are found in the house. They look for them in the garden; in the palace of their god-father Núñez Vela, who lives so close; and they look in the streets of the city. All their efforts seem useless: the children don't appear anywhere. There is a very uneasy feeling in the house, as their parents are terribly worried about the whereabouts of the two children. Maybe they left the city while playing and they got lost; maybe some house servant or some Jew...

After several hours of anxiety, the brother of Mr. Alonso, Franciso de Cepeda, knocks at the door. He has arrived on his horse carrying Teresa in front and Rodrigo behind him. He found them far from the city walls, towards the northeast, past the bridge which crosses the River Adaja, and close to a monument of four granite columns. According to them, they were on journey to "the land of the moors" so that they would be decapitated by them as martyrs, and so be able to go straight to heaven like them, in the midst of angels, crowns and canticles. They both return sadly. Their uncle has made their fabulous dream wither away as a rose, right next to the River Adaja, the granite city walls still within sight, and so close —as the two children thought— to "the land of the moors", where the martyrs gain their glory at the easy price of martyrdom.

* * *

FLOS SANCTORUM used by Saint Teresa.

But Teresa isn't discouraged. One dream withers away and another crops up much stronger. If they can't be martyrs, they'll be hermits, like those of which they had read in the lives of the saints. And so they put themselves to work. Everyday, holding hands firmly, Teresa and Rodrigo go out to the garden of stone walls. And they play; they play in the midst of songs and dust. Rodrigo looks throughout the garden for small rocks, odd pieces of brick, and he takes them to Teresa who, sitting on the ground, strives to construct some walls, trying to make them appear with windows. It's a hermitage. They're playing "hermits". When they see it finished, they start jumping and clapping, delirious with joy for the job well done. Then they recite their devotions, their readings, they have their prayer time with their small hands united together on their chest and their eyes looking toward heaven. And they start to dream: if the little animals would come to rest humbly before them as they had read in the lives of the hermits...!

With great enthusiasm, the next day they return to the garden to continue their practices next to their little hermitage. But... what a shame! It has fallen down. The two little children look silently and disappointedly at the ruins of the small house they had made the day before. A bit of wind that had blown during the night had pushed the mud and rocks to the ground.

THE FOUR POSTS. The monument found on the road from Avila to Salamanca, at a very short distance from the city. It was here where Teresa and Rodrigo, while escaping to the land of the moors, were surprised by their uncle Francisco, who returned them to their home.

AMADIS DE GAULA. The 1515 edition, printed in Medina del Campo.

CHAPTER II

FICTION NOVELS AND FEMININE DRESSING

In these years, Spain is full of its desire for adventure and conquest. Avila, land of knights and crusaders, still treasures the recent memory of the last battles, when Jimena Blázquez defended the city with its women dressed as soldiers behind the parapets of the city walls. Through its streets the sound of the spurs and swords of the warriors who depart to Flanders or to the recently discovered America can be heard continuously.

And the popular literature lives from this as well. In the evenings in the palaces and the noble houses, alternating with books of piety, they read the history of battles, stories of fantastic adventures and the narration of the heroic deeds of the knights. In the Cepeda house, Mrs. Beatriz de Ahumada enjoys reading them and looks at them as an innocent entertainment and a distraction from her worries.

One day those books fall into the hands of Teresa and Rodrigo. They come with laminas of battles, of walking knights, of gallants and of ladies finely dressed and perfumed. Teresa gets dazzled by it all. It seems so attractive to be able to give a pleasant appearance and to feel loved by others like those fiction ladies…! And she starts to imitate them.

She no longer goes to the garden to play with Rodrigo the hermit game; she no longer looks to heaven repeating "forever, and ever, and ever!" She likes to look at herself in the mirror, to take care of her hair curls, to pamper her fine hands, to put perfume on… If before she dreamed about being a hermit or about dying for Christ in the hands of the moors, now she is concerned about being looked at and admired by the dressy gallants when they pass below the entrance gate of Alcázar.

And at home, she no longer talks about the martyrdoms or of the life of penitents; now her discourse is on hobbies, dressing up, and gallants. A young and "worldly" relative of hers, begins initiating her in the most frivolous feminine ways. They pass a lot of time together chatting and whispering behind the back of her mother, who isn't happy with the friendships of her daughter. It all leads to a point in which Teresa finds herself in a world of ideas, desires and fantasies very different to those of her first years. Her cousins have led her there by the hand.

But it's not only her young relative that has made Teresa interest herself in that brilliant world of lights, fashions and perfumes: it has also been a son of her uncle Mr. Francisco de Cepeda. The house in which he lives so close that there is only a wall between them, and the wall has a small door that opens up to passageway between the two houses. So they go from one house to the other whenever they please. They play and make jokes together in the garden and in the living rooms. The cousin doesn't separate himself from Teresa, so intelligent and pleasant to be with, who knows how to give life to their conversations and games, and so, there comes a day in which the friendship of the cousin grows into something more. Teresa is thirteen years old. She is full of charm, life and elegance. But she doesn't have and entirely insensible heart. She loves him and she lets herself be loved. They talk alone in the shadows of the family living room, dimly lit by the oil-lamp, and they even plan, for later on, their happy matrimonial union at the foot of the altar of the parish church.

* * *

A sad occurrence disturbs the joy of Mr. Alonso's house: Mrs. Beatriz de Ahumada has died. This happens in the last few days of 1528. When this sad news reaches the Cepeda house from Gotarrendura, the small town in which she had died on the northwest of Avila, twenty kilometres from the city, it produces a painful shock in the household. Teresa cries inconsolably while embracing her older brothers who unsuccessfully try to maintain themselves strong before this terrible blow that breaks so many hopes, and kills so many joys. It is the first strong pain that visits them, and they all grieve profoundly. They have lost their mother, still young and beautiful, so good, so affectionate...

The next day, a funeral procession slowly advances from Gotarrendura towards Avila. A heavy cart carries the coffin with the corpse of Mrs. Beatriz de Ahumada. Behind them, right next to the bodily remains of his wife, Mr. Alonso follows, sad and downcast, but serene. On each side, there are relatives, friends and household servants, who pray in silence for the diseased.

The procession advances along difficult and winding roads; some going up and others going down. They travel on the snow which covers as a veil all that rough land full of peaked rocks. And they finally arrive at Avila; recollected and in silence they cross the Roman bridge over the river; and they enter the western entrance of the city wall. When Teresa and her brothers discover the funeral procession while peeking from the windows left ajar, and they see the coffin in which

OUR LADY OF CHARITY. "When my mother died I was twelve years of age, or a little younger. As I began to understand what I had lost, heartbroken, to went before an image of Our Lady and I pleaded her with many tears to be my mother" (*Life* 1, 7). Today, the image is venerated in the Cathedral of Avila.

their Mother is being carried, they break out into tears and sobs as a sad farewell of the children to their good mother who leaves them forever.

A little while later, Teresa is seen leaving the house alone, silently crossing the streets to go to the eastern part of the city. She goes down through the suburb of the Jews, crying; she goes out through the city wall and enters into the chapel of Saint Lawrence, on the right side of the river. She prostrates herself at the foot of the statue of Our Lady of Grace. Before her, sobbing and weeping, she pours out all the pain of her broken heart. She feels as though she had a great weight on her chest. Everything seems gloomy for her. With her dead mother, it was as though they had buried her enthusiasm and her joy of living. Her heart feels empty and broken, as though it had a big hollow in it, wide and profound, as a pit left by a tree torn out, roots and all. And she asks Our Lady to help and comfort her. She alone can make the flowers and the lilies on the road of her life flourish again, now that she offers herself to her, feeling so tired, sad and wearisome...

*   *   *

Teresa grows in grace and beauty as well as in age. Fifteen, sixteen, seventeen years old. The days and months that have passed by, have dimmed the pain of losing her mother, and Mr. Alonso's lovely daughter keeps in contact with her cousin, she keeps taking care of her gentle hands, perfuming her hair and dresses, walking through the streets and plazas with her beauty and elegance, provoking admiration and affection towards her wherever she goes.

Her father pays careful attention to the sort of friendships that his daughter has, as he is well aware that she is still in the effervescence of her youth, of her beauty and of her inexperience. The noble gentleman is not pleased with the relationship with the relative that visits their home, and that is becoming evermore intimate.

"I had some first cousins... who were about my age, maybe a little older. We spent a lot of time together" (Life 2, 2).

At night time, when the family is at home alone, Mr. Alonso, with love and affection, calls Teresa to attention, advising her against those long conversations with her cousin. Teresa responds with silence, but the next day they return to their whispering, dates and interminable conversations. Then, her father has to warn her again, and so does her elder sister. But it's worthless. It seems as though Teresa no longer has control over her heart that leads her irremissibly toward the son of Mr. Francisco de Cepeda. At least, that is what Mr. Alonso concludes, and he decides to break, once and for all, the occasion and the danger.

It's the 13th of July of 1531. At the Cepeda home there are emotional farewells and goodbye kisses. Teresa leaves with Mr. Alonso; they cross the small square in front of the Núñez Vela house; they pass below the arch of the city wall entrance, and on the left, they start walking down an alleyway that goes towards the west, parallel to the city walls. After about five minutes walking in a straight line, between the city walls on the left, and the southern suburb on the right, father and daughter find themselves, after a going down a steep incline, before a poor convent of nuns. They are the "Augustinians of Grace".

OUR LADY OF GRACE. It is in this monastery of Augustinian nuns where Teresa stayed a little more than a year as a student, living the internal boarding regimen.

Mr. Alonso speaks with the Mother Superior. He wants Teresa to enter there as student in an internal boarding regimen, isolated from any exterior contact, without any visits of friends or correspondence with relatives, and above all, isolation from that cousin that loves her and goes after her. When Mr. Alonso says goodbye to his daughter, who is left inside the convent and the door closed behind her, he discretely wipes a tear from his eye: it's the first time that he is left alone, separated from his beloved daughter. But he believes it is necessary, and the noble Castillian gentleman, with a firm and steady pace, climbs the small incline next to the city wall, and pensively returns to the family home.

Teresa, who was quite sad the first few days in her new life as an internal boarder, bit by bit starts to change her attitude thanks to the affectionate attention of the nuns, who have taken to her. She even gets to feel very happy in the agreeable atmosphere of the nun's college. The joy and life of the other young boarders, the college classes, the new order of life that has an occupation for each hour and moment of the day, make the nostalgia of the family home and of the company of her brothers fade away. Sometimes she still thinks of her cousin, a thought that he tries to maintain and keep alive by sending messages and letters through the turn. But these messages don't always fall into the hands of Teresa. With the passing of time, and so many new experiences, the memory of him and those other dreams, dim away.

1. **AVILA.** Façade of the church of the saint, constructed on the site where the house in which she was born was located.

    The "house of money", where Teresa was born on the 28th of March of 1515 and where she lived the first twenty years of her life, bordering on the north with the church of Saint Dominic, today totally lost; in front is the wall of the city, and on the west is the hospital of Saint Scholastica and the palace of Núñez Vela, constructed during her infancy.

2. The palace of Núñez Vela.

3. The façade of the hospital of Saint Scholastica (in its actual state).

THE MARTYRIAL ROUTE:

4. The sepulchre of the martyrs of Avila: Vincent, Sabina and Cristeta, in the Basilica of Saint Vincent.
5. Roman bridge that crosses the River Adaja.
6. The stained glass window that represents this Teresian adventure of the quest for martyrdom, in the natal house of the saint.

4

5

6

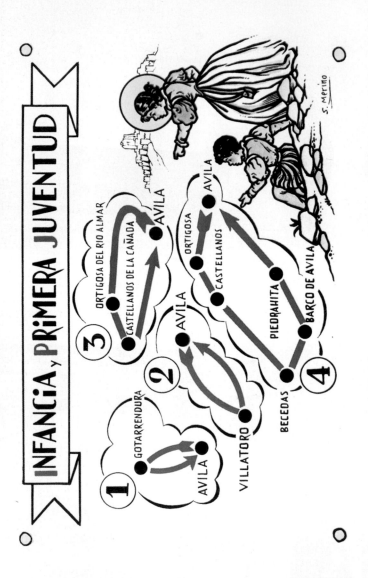

7. VILLATORO, one of the villages visited by Teresa on her way to the wedding of her sister Mary (1531).

GEOGRAFIA TERESIANA

PROVINCIA DE AVILA

a
Salamanca

● Duruelo

PROVINCIA DE SALAMANCA

● Castellanos
de la Cañada

● Piedrahita

Becedas

El Barco de Avila

PROVINCIA DE CACERES

PROV

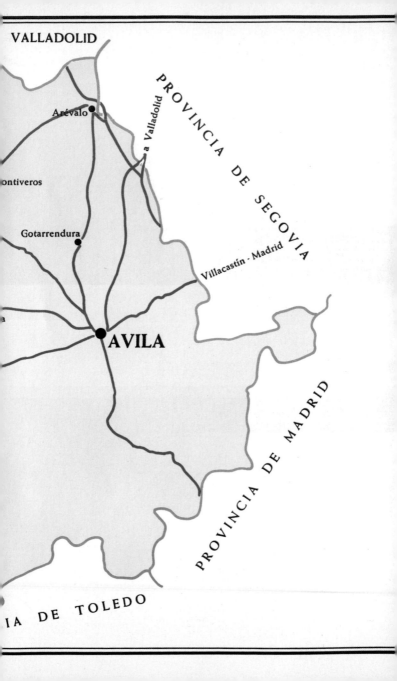

8

9

**GEOGRAPHY
OF A PASSIONATE
ADOLESCENCE:**

10

11

12. AVILA. Saint Mary of Grace.

13. CASTELLANOS DE LA CAÑADA (Avila). Landscape.

14. ORTIGOSA (Avila). Palace of Mr. Pedro de Cepeda. The entrance (today blocked up) and the shield of a noble.

15. The parish church of Ortigosa.

One day, Mary Briceno, Mistress of the young boarder girls, talks to them about the calling to life in the cloister. The Augustinian nun tells the story of how she herself felt Gods calling. Her college students listen with all ears, following the fantastic narration with eyes wide open. It had been the fruit of an incidental reading she had made. Her eyes fell on a book with the following Gospel passage: "Many are called, but few are chosen", and this was the beam of light she needed to make her realise the vanity of life and the dangers of the world. Teresa, who follows attentively the vocation story, feels as though the ideals and interests of her childhood, that had been lying dormant within her, were now being reborn with the good readings and spiritual talks. But she hadn't yet discovered her religious vocation. She was a declared enemy of the idea of being a nun.

THE CONVENT OF THE INCARNATION. Façade.
Engraving of the nineteenth century.

CHAPTER III

TO THE CONVENT
OF THE INCARNATION

Avila has dressed itself up. It's a beautiful day of May in 1534. Before the entrance gate of Alcázar there are arcs of triumph, and waving flags and pennants on the parapets of the homage tower. The nobles of the city and gentlemen on their well harnessed horses come and go beneath the big stone arch: saddles bordered with gold, spurs of silver, shining helmets with feathers, sparkling swords, damascene shields... And at each side, there are finely dressed girls, radiating enthusiasm and beauty.

The vibrating kettle drums and horns are sounding. It is the announcement of the arrival of the Emperor. And below a canopy of gold, the royal figure of Charles V appears mounted on his horse and smiling as a grand lord toward the multitude of people that acclaim him. The artillery

sounds clear. There is a moment of silence and
expectation. The young monarch takes off his
bonnet, and with his right hand placed on the
Gospels, he swears aloud that he will uphold the
privileges and exemptions conceded to the
ancient and noble Castillian city. The Governor
of the fortress then approaches and offers him
the keys to the city on an engraved silver plate.
The artillery salute is heard once more as well as
the acclamations from the crowd, and the Emper-
or enters below the stone arch of flowers into the
interior of the fortified part of the city, while the
people stay outside cheering enthusiastically.
Then there is bullfighting, and the playing of typical festive games with horses and lances. During
various days, all of Avila vibrates with the celebration of the imperial visit.

Among the beautiful young girls of Avila who
acclaim Charles V and applaud joyfully, is the nine-
teen year old Teresa de Ahumada in the plenitude
of her youth. She participates in the popular festivities as well as going for walks and meeting up
with her friends. But beneath all of this, she is
going through a kind of interior spiritual battle
which deadens the joy of those jubilant festivities.

Two years have gone by since she left the College of Grace due to an illness which made her
travel to Castellanos de la Cañada. On her way, she
stopped in the town of Hortigosa, where her uncle,
Mr. Pedro de Cepeda lived. On this occasion, he
gave her some religious books that awoke in her
an inclination to the life in the cloister. These sen-

Patrimonio Nacional mantiene abierta la visita pública en:

MADRID: Palacio Real y Jardines del Campo del Moro. Palacio Real de El Pardo. Reales Monasterios y Conventos de Las Descalzas y La Encarnación. Panteón de Hombres Ilustres.

PROVINCIA DE MADRID: San Lorenzo de El Escorial: Real Monasterio. Aranjuez: Palacio Real y Jardines. Real Casa del Labrador, Museo de Faluas Reales.

PROVINCIA DE SEGOVIA. San Ildefonso: Palacio Real y Jardines de La Granja. Palacio Real y Bosque de Riofrío.

BURGOS: Real Monasterio de Santa María la Real de Huelgas.

PROVINCIA DE VALLADOLID. Tordesillas: Real Convento de Santa Clara.

PALMA DE MALLORCA: Palacio Real de la Almudaina.

PROVINCIA DE CACERES: Cuacos de Yuste: Monasterio de Yuste.

PATRIMONIO NACIONAL

PALACIO REAL DE MADRID

www.patrimonionacional.es
Teléfono: (+34) 91 454 88 00

Consérvese el Billete hasta la salida del recinto.

timents fight against the horror she had always felt toward the idea of being a nun. It's a fight between a religious vocation and life in the world. She already knows what the life of a nun is like, from what she saw in the College of Grace, and she also knows what life in the world is like. The first option seems to her a negation of pleasures, the renunciation of comforts, a kind of burial of the plenitude of her youth. The second option seems to be the very opposite: the loving care of relatives, praises of fortune and from men, parties with bullfights, tournaments and games. But, what happens when all of this comes to an end...? At the end of an austere and mortified life in the cloister, comes heaven, and at the end of the pleasures and fun-times that the world promises, maybe it's hell that is awaiting her. And inside of Teresa, those words, which had made such an impact on her when she was small and that she had repeated so often with her little brother Rodrigo in the home garden when they read the lives of the saints, came back to her mind: "forever! and ever! and ever...!"

* * *

Yet another blow is going to convince Teresa even more of the vanity of life: the farewell of her brother Rodrigo. It is autumn of 1535. Her confident of games, fervours and childhood pranks leaves her, possibly forever. The young Cepeda feels, as so many Spanish people did, that the blood of war and conquest flows through his veins, and he wants to embark on boat to America. One fine day, he farewells his father and his brothers. When Teresa sees him leave for Seville, she feels as though one of the most dear dreams of her heart has been broken. It seems as if all that she holds dear is to be taken from her! First it was her mother, who was taken to the grave; then it was her sister Maria, who left the family home to get married; now Rodrigo, who is leaving to never return. The unreliability of the things of the world becomes evident to her.

At the same time, her appreciation of all that is eternal, increases in her. At home, she dedicates long hours to the reading of the epistles of St. Jerome, which proclaim the excellence of the spiritual life and ponder the pre-eminence of the religious vocation. The severe language, full of energy and warmth, of the grand Father of the Church, impresses the young and beautiful daughter of Mr. Alonso, who, bit by bit, begins detaching herself from the lovely dresses and other vanities. She no longer likes to walk near the arch of Alcázar to flaunt her beauty, where the youth socialize and laugh happily among silk garments and perfume. She prefers to pass hours in the church, to nurture her spiritual needs with the theologians of the College of St. Tomas, to visit nun's convents.

THE CONVENT OF THE INCARNATION. Teresa lived here for thirty years. The whole convent is full of remembrances of her. Each stone is a relic; each corner, a chapter of her life.

Some time ago, a friend of hers, Juana Juárez, took the Carmelite habit in the Convent of the Incarnation. At that time, Teresa was horrified by the idea of her friend entering the cloister. But now, it didn't seem so strange to her, and she even starts to visit her frequently. Many days, she is seen leaving the city walls through the Carmen gate; going down the hill northward; crossing the small River Ajates by the stone bridge and entering into the parlour of the Incarnation. She is wearing an orange dress with black velvet borders. A little while later, the nun comes to the grill, and there, Juana Juárez on the inside, Teresa on the outside, they spend a lot of time talking, sometimes about things of an indifferent nature, but mostly on spiritual and mystical topics.

When the beautiful daughter of Mr. Alonso returns home, everyone notices that she is more recollected, that she seems more withdrawn and concerned. The conversations in the parlour of the Incarnation with Juana Juárez, and the reading of the letters of St. Jerome, have the effect of settling the religious vocation in her spirit. In favour and against; conveniences and inconveniences; pros and cons; all these considerations are going round in the head of the charming young girl, who finds herself between two worlds.

In the end she becomes convinced, and after the conviction, the decision: an unbreakable decision, that no one will be able to bend. She will be a nun. God wants it so. It is also the way to secure her salvation. What are all the other reasons and difficulties next to this?

The biggest of these difficulties is her father. The noble figure of Mr. Alonso, now quite elderly, almost abandoned by as many children as he has brought up, stands between Teresa and the convent. He is not resigned to separate himself from his most precious daughter, the joy of his heart, the flower and smile of the yellowed autumn of his life. Without her, the only thing that he would have left would be the black and empty grave, waiting to embrace him with its soil, and sink him into its cold night.

But Teresa knows that God calls her, and she'll even have to overcome the pain of her dear father. He that calls her, will have to provide the consolation for the person that she loves most on earth. On her behalf, she will save him from the pain of the farewell. Before he knows, she is already in the convent, and she is confident that he won't try to get her out by force. She plans it, and she puts it into action.

It's an October morning. Mr. Alonso is still sleeping alone in his bedroom. Several hours will have to pass before the sun enlightens the towers of the castles and the parapets of the city walls. But Teresa is already moving stealthily along the corridors; she opens and closes the cupboards and doors as carefully as possible, trying to evade any kind of noise; she dresses herself and fixes up her room. Then she opens the outside door, and steps into the silent and cold street. She takes the corner between the St. Scholastica and St. Dominic's Parish Church, and she follows the road towards the northern part of the city. Her small and speedy footsteps resound in the silence of the winding and frozen streets. Sometimes she looks back, as though afraid that someone might be following her. She passes in front of the doors of the convent of Carmen, she leaves the city walls, goes down the hill, leaving on her right the narrow St. Martin's tower, and passing over the small Ajates' bridge, se finds herself before the doors of the Convent of the Incarnation. The day begins to dawn. When Teresa looks back towards the city, that has been left silent, asleep, she sees the shadow of the rigid and austere city walls that the rising sun begins to highlight on the background of the brightening blue sky.

CHAPTER IV

A NUN WITH A WHITE CAPE

The Incarnation, with church and convent, forms a simple and spacious building, which is situated in the north of Avila, outside the city walls, about five hundred metres from the city. It has a central patio with a small well, and rose bushes; it has a spacious garden with trees; it has cloisters with stone arcs that give entrance to the small but joyful interior garden, and in the midst of all of this, there nearly two hundred nuns with white capes moving around.

The second of November, 1536: the cold day of the souls. In the city the sad tolling of the bells are heard as they call for prayers for the dead. But in the Incarnation, there is hustle and the joyfulness of celebration. The church and the choir are decorated with flowers, and the sweet little convent bell swings happily in the humble bell tower of three arcs. There is a small group coming down the hill from the city formed by Mr.

Alonso de Cepeda, his relatives, his friends and some young people. They are coming to Teresa's ceremony of the taking of the Carmelite habit.

The novice's father and the participants take seat in the church next to the grill of the lower choir. The small curtain is opened, and there in the inside of the cloisters, at first at a distance, then closer, the angelical voices of the nuns is heard. A little while later, they enter into the choir two by two. They enter with their white capes and the veil over their faces. At the end of the procession, while they sing the last stanzas of the liturgical hymn, Teresa enters accompanied by the Prioress and the Mistress of novices. Hundreds of enthusiastic eyes are fixed on her, looking through the choir grill. She enters recollected and full of emotion, in all white, as a virgin in her wedding dress: her eyes look down, and the expression on her face is slightly affected by the emotion and the sweet and chaste smile that timidly appears on her lips.

When she prostrates herself before the Mother Prioress, who is seated in the centre, and the vesting of the habit goes ahead, Mr. Alonso, who follows the ceremony full of emotion, from the other side of the grill, feels an inner motion, a kind of a shiver down his spine. His adorable daughter, full of youth and beauty, dressed with the whitecape of Our Lady of Carmel! If her mother, who loved her so much, were still alive! The noble gentleman wipes away a small tear that has silently escaped from his eyes and gently falls down his cheeks.

Afterwards, once the warm ceremony has finished, all is converted into joyfulness and good wishes throughout the cloisters and parlours for the new nun.

* * *

After so much happiness and festivities in the convent, where they had enjoyed a specially prepared meal for the occasion, wax candles and new veils for the nuns, all gifts to the community given by Mr. Alonso according to the custom of the convent, Teresa begins her noviciate. She is happy in her new life. She has a spacious and well lit cell, with views of the city: she can see the walls, the parapets, the towers, the bell towers; and with splendid views of the mountainous countryside and of the river; she has religious nuns that appreciate her very much, like Juana Juárez; she receives frequent visits from relatives and friends, who come to see her in the Incarnation and keep her amused in the parlour.

And the spiritual life is practised by her with the fervours of a beginner. Prayer; readings and monastic instructions with the Mistress of novices; rehearsing prayers, hymns and ceremonies; the practice of virtues: that is the day in the life of the young and sweet little nun, who feels in her soul all the attraction of an intense spiritual rebirth. Sometimes the penance of the Order seems little for her, and she looks for sting-

ing nettle shrubs to mortify her flesh in the retreat
of her cell and in the solitude of the night.

*   *   *

But one day, Teresa doesn't appear in the community acts. At the cloister door, Mr. Alonso
Sánchez de Cepeda is waiting for her impatiently
and worried. The doctors and surgeons have
entered. The nuns are moving backwards and for-
wards through the cloisters and corridors carrying white cloths, bandages and medicines. Teresa
is in a grave state. She is stretched out on the bed
of her cell unconscious, as though she no longer
existed: rigid hands, eyes closed, a wax colour on
her face. When the doctors leave, her father, who
was awaiting the result of the visit and of the examination, hears the medical diagnosis: her daughter has suffered a heart attack, and she needs a
treatment that cannot be administered to her in
the convent. It will be necessary to take her out.
Maybe a folk healer, famous in the province, who
lives in a small village town in the mountains, will
find a solution to this terrible sickness.

Mr. Alonso, alarmed, doesn't consider it twice,
and decides to put his daughter into the hands of
the folk healer. He doesn't care about the cost or
the difficulties. No expense is too great to save
the life of his adorable daughter Teresa.

It's the beginning of winter. In Avila, it snows
during the day and freezing winds blow throughout the night. The oak trees, whitened with frost,

seem to be almond trees in flower. The streets and roads are hard and slippery because of the ice. The city, stiff with cold and still covered in shadows, conserves a kind of sacred recollection, and its streets, recollected in the walls, seem to convert themselves into cloisters and corridors of an immense monastery of the Middle Ages.

Warmly dressed up, and mounted on good horses, a small group crosses the bridge over the River Adaja and goes up on an inclined road westward. There are six or seven of them: Teresa and her father, Sister Juana Juárez and some of the household servants. They go in search of the famous healer. Mr. Alonso's daughter, who has just left the Incarnation, is weak and with a fever, very sick from the last heart attacks that she has suffered. They cross the plain, where a freezing wind seems to blow through to the bone. Mr. Alonso, who always travels close aside to his daughter's horse, makes sure that she is well wrapt up, asking frequently how she is. And they travel in this way one league after another along the winding and narrow roads flanked by rocks and bramble bushes.

When they get to Castellanos de la Cañada, a small town of twelve houses, there are two people awaiting them: Mrs. María de Cepeda, Teresa's eldest sister, and her husband, Mr. Martín Guzmán Barrientos. Teresa arrives quite fatigued, with feverish shivers and generally ridden down by weakness. How good will the stop here be for her on the way to Becedas! A stop which would be much longer than they had expected and would have wanted.

There's a problem. The folk healer won't be able to start the treatment until the cold weather has passed, and they're still at the beginning of winter. But she'll be well there: attended with care, without worries, pampered by all. On her behalf, Teresa makes the best of her time there, sanctifying herself in the pain of her illness, reading spiritual books and dedicating herself to prayer, which flows from her soul now with more emotion than ever.

* * *

The winter cold has now past. The fields are losing their red ploughed colour and acquire emerald green tonalities. The bramble bushes on the boundaries begin to sprout up with small leaves and long stems, as though they were stretching themselves after being shrugged up for so many months by the cold. The grass begins to timidly peep out onto the tepid atmosphere of the fields, with yearning to receive the sweet warmth of the spring sun. The time has come in which the folk healer of Becedas works her charms. Mr. Alonso, his daughter, Juana Juárez and the servants, leave Castellanos de la Cañada in search for the small town of the prodigious woman healer.

The mountain range of Avila and Salamanca, on the foothills of Gredos: that is where Becedas is, lifted on a hill from where the typical Avila scenery and village fields can be seen. It is a beautiful village with six streets, two plazas and four fountains, which pour out pure and healthy mountain water.

It has textile looms to make woollen garments and linen cloth, weavers and windmills. It has oak wood, fruit and pastures that are watered by four streams that come from the Tormes river.

This is where the famous healer lives. Mr. Alonso looks for her with vehement enthusiasm as though expecting to find in her the complete solution to all their worries. That woman, as they had told him, is the only person that can save his adorable daughter.

The treatment begins: first comes the daily purges; then the mysterious potions; always medications without measure, that the healer prepares with herbs and ground roots in her poor mud-brick house. And the patient gets sicker and sicker. Her temperature rises, the heart attacks continue and are becoming stronger each time, and the lack of appetite increase with each potion that the woman healer makes her take. Three months go by, and the fabulous treatment is destroying Teresa. Instead of curing her heart problem, it damages her lungs. Mr. Alonso, who came with so much faith and enthusiasm, in the end, looses his trust in the mysterious healer and decides to return with his daughter to Avila. In this way, at least she will die in her father's house.

And in the month of June, they leave Becedas, which is left in the beauty of its hills, pastures and streams, and they return, sad and disappointed, to their walled city. How long and how hostile does the road now seem to them, that before they had travelled with so much enthusiasm for the desired miracle!

* * *

In the cloister of stone arcs, that leads to the central patio of the Incarnation, there is an open grave. The nuns have prepared black altar cloths, and they prepare the catafalque in the church surrounded by large funeral candles. It is all awaiting the body of Teresa de Ahumada, who has already been unconscious for four days in her father's house. She had a strong heart attack, and they haven't been able to make her come round. Relatives, friends and nuns from the Incarnation watch over her. Even the wax from the big candles which glow around her bed has fallen on her eyelids, but she still hasn't responded. They are all quite sure that she is dead: everyone except her father, who repeats in the funeral atmosphere of the bedroom a last cry of hope: "This daughter isn't to be buried!"

CHAPTER V

PATERNAL ORPHANAGE

In the first parlour of the Incarnation, seated on the other side of the grill, there is a venerable old man waiting silently and recollectedly. A sweet twilight floods the small brick floored room with plastered walls and dark wooden beams in the ceiling. The little light that enters, comes through a high grilled window which opens onto the exterior patio, and makes it possible to recognise the man: it is Mr. Alonso Sánchez de Cepeda. He is worried, downcast, and in deep thought.

The opening of a door is heard on the inside and Mr. Alonso looks up, to fix his gaze on the darkness that envelopes the other side of the iron grill. And he smiles. He begins to distinguish his daughter, who approaches. She comes with two religious who sustain her, one on each side, because Teresa has been left crippled since the last terrible paroxysm that had her with one foot in the grave. They sit her on a seat, and the nursing nuns let her be. Father and daughter are left alone. Mr. Alonso smiles sweetly and sadly, while Teresa tells him, with enthusiasm and optimism, about the slow recovery from her illness that she is experimenting.

Then they talk about the spiritual life, about prayer, about recollection, about God. Teresa, whose virtues have grown a lot during these last two years of physical suffering, initiates her father in the practice of mental prayer. She has learnt it from the *Third Alphabet* of the master Osuna, a precious book that her uncle Mr. Pedro de Cepeda had put in her hands during her stay in Hortigosa. She speaks to him of the benefits of the practice of it, the graces God concedes in it, the strength it gives to the soul, and the help it provides in the practice of the virtues. The holy old man listens enchanted by his daughter as though he were listening to an angel from heaven who was revealing to him mysteries from another world, and he promises her that he will dedicate himself with constancy in the practice that Teresa describes in such an extraordinary way.

When the noble gentleman leaves the Incarnation and climbs the little hill that leads to the entrance of Carmen of the city walls, he carries some books with him: his daughter has given them to him through the turn so that they may help him in his mental prayer.

*   *   *

Teresa is no longer crippled. One day she entrusted her sickness to Saint Joseph, and she has seen the protection of the Patriarchal saint in the rapid disappearance of her pains and in the agility of her numbed members. Now she can walk along the cloisters and go to the parlour without the help of other nuns. And throughout the convent the joyful voice and the contagious laugh of Teresa is heard once again. She returns to her role of inspiring enthusiasm and happiness among the nuns, who laugh along with the daughter of Mr. Alonso de Cepeda. The pains, and the appearance of premature exhaustion have disappeared, and even her heart, almost torn apart by the terrible attacks, has recuperated all the energy and ardour that corresponds to her youth, that hasn't yet disappeared.

She feels a certain need for affection and to renew her enthusiasm. She spends hours and hours in the parlour telling funny and wonderful things in exciting conversations that seem to endure indefinitely! Stuck to the grill, her eyes sparkle with interest. And that is why a young nobleman of Avila, enchanted by her, starts to come down from the city to visit and spend a lot of time talking to the delightful nun, contemplating the attractive face, with three beauty spots, of Teresa de Ahumada, maybe with the intention of gaining her heart so as to make her leave the voluntary enclosure that she is in.

Life seems to smile on her again; the memories of her youthful adventures flood back to her imagination; human affection comes back to look

for a small sunlit corner in the heart of the beautiful daughter of Mr. Alonso; below the religious
habit the ardent heart of this extraordinary
woman begins to stir once again.

But a sad happening is going to freeze the smile
on her lips, is going to put tears in her eyes, and is
going to cover, with a mourning cloak, the desires
that have hardly begun to flourish in her heart.

* * *

It is the 26th of December, 1544. Christmas cel-
ebrations without joy in the Cepeda house. While
in the streets, drums and Christmas carols are
heard, Mr. Alonso dictates his last testament from
his bedroom. His brother Mr. Lorenzo de Cepeda, the priest from Villanueva del Aceral, his son-
in-law Martín Guzmán Barrientos and his sons
are there, next to his bed. Teresa, who has come
from the Incarnation, stands out from the rest
with her Carmelite habit.

Everyone in the room listens solemnly to the
dignified and serene voice of Mr. Alonso. The
notary transcribes the last will of the dying gentleman. The others, sad, downcast, with their
eyes blurred by tears, pray in silence. The name
of Teresa is heard, and his voice shakes while pro-
nouncing, maybe for the last time, the name of
his adorable daughter. Then there is a long and

THE PARLOUR OF THE INCARNATION.

anxious silence. The sick man breaths with difficulty. But he makes an effort and talks again, but
now with more emotion, with tears in his eyes:
"Everything comes to an end —Mr. Alonso says
on the threshold of eternity— only one thing
remains: having served Our Lord". And the noble
gentleman laments not having surrendered his
life to God in the enclosure of a convent of the
most strict and penitent observance. There is
silence once again in the room; the sobs and sighs
are contained. The sick man makes another effort
to talk: "I believe in God the Father Almighty, Cre-
ator of heaven and earth..." He is unable to continue. His voice dyes away, and a wax colour slowly extends throughout his face and his hands, that
have been left on top of the bed. He has expired.
Everyone falls to their knees: prayers of petition
and of tears, which accompany the immortal
spirit in its ascension to glory.

CHAPTER VI

DREAMS OF A FOUNDRESS

Throughout Avila, there is talk of a nun in the Incarnation who has ecstasies, raptures and visions of angels. She plans to make a foundation of discalced nuns. They talk about it at the doors of the churches, in the evening suppers in the noble houses, in the convents. Even from the pulpit they make scathing allusions to the presumptuous nun that pretends to be a foundress. And they mutter the name: Teresa de Ahumada.

Some laugh. She was well known in the city from her youthful years of socialising; they had seen her appear on the streets perfumed, with her fine and small hands well manicured, carefully done hair, and they certainly don't think she has the qualities that are required to found convents. Others condemn her without knowing her at all. They don't see anything in this but a desire to stand out and to be considered a saint. Some think that it is a case which the Inquisition should investigate, because it seems to them, that all this talk of a foundation can only be dreams of a deluded visionary, and so-called miracle-working nun. Only some very few, those who have dealt with her spiritually and have knowledge of her intimate life, think that there is a lot more than the mere whim of an overexcited woman. They know of her tried virtues, of her humility, of her spirit of prayer and penance. During twenty years she has dedicated herself to an intense spiritual life, she is detached from all earthy affection thanks to her strength of spirit and constancy. But even these few friends look upon the idea of the foundation with doubts. Convinced that she is well intentioned, they think, nonetheless, that it's a crazy idea. Even her confessor, a Jesuit, is doubtful, and perplexed.

*   *   *

One day the people that gather to socialise near the entrance of Alcázar look curiously at a nun and a lady who pass across the main square. There is murmuring and bad intentioned laughter. They are Mother Teresa and Mrs. Guiomar de Ulloa, the foundresses. They are going down the Amblés valley and are heading toward St. Thomas' College. They are looking for a theologian to present their projects to. Mrs. Guiomar talks about the income that they count on to maintain the convent, and Mother Teresa explains the spirit and the purposes of the foundation. A Dominican Friar —with a white habit, a penetrating gaze, a firm and precise manner of speech— listens attentively to the plans and responds to the questions they ask. Father Pedro Ibáñez doesn't condemn the idea straight away, as many had already done. Their intentions, he thinks, are good; the idea, is holy; the plans, are well orientated to the glory of God and the salvation of souls. But he abstains from giving a definitive answer. It is a serious matter, and so he asks for eight days to think about it before giving his opinion as a theologian.

Eight days later, the foundresses return. They have prayed a lot, putting their plans and projects in the hands of God. And have decided to attend to the decision of the Dominican Friar as if it were an order from heaven. If he disapproves, they will abandon the idea to occupy themselves exclusively with their own sanctification. If he approves, they will dedicate all their energies to make it a reality, even if everyone else condemns and murmurs against them.

And the opinion of the theologian is enthusiastically in favour. "If anyone goes against it —he tells them as they leave— let them come to me, and I will convince them". When Mother Teresa leaves the Dominican College with Mrs. Guiomar, and they set out to climb the hill toward the city, their eyes are radiating joy: it was as though a big weight had been lifted from them; rays of light transform the grey horizon into sunshine. The approval of the theologian of St. Thomas' is for

them light and hope in the midst of so much con-
demnation, ridicule and contempt that had been
mixing up their plans and even in their own personal lives.

* * *

From this moment, the activity of Mother Teresa increases. She acts decisively, and knows how
to defend herself before those who oppose her.
She speaks to the Bishop, to Saint Peter of Alcántara, to the Provincial of the Carmelites. She looks
everywhere for advice and help for the small convent of her hopes that is slowly taking shape.

But there are still many ups and downs to overcome. The confessor approves one day, and disapproves the next; the Provincial enthusiastically promises to help decisively, and at the hour of
truth, he backs away; even the Bishop, who never had doubts about Mother Teresa or her work,
vacillates about the character and conditions that
the foundation should have. There comes a time
in which Teresa finds herself with her hands tied:
the confessor has prohibited her to occupy herself with the project. Not even one step more. The
saint obeys, and she recollects herself in her cell
in the Incarnation.

THE MONASTERY OF SAINT THOMAS. Among the
Dominican Fathers of this convent, Teresa found her best
friends and the most faithful defenders of her Reform.

On top of this, a little while later, Mother Teresa is sent to Toledo for almost seven months to help Mrs. Luisa de la Cerda, a noble lady resident there to accept God's will in the midst of certain difficulties.

However, the project for the foundation goes ahead. Mrs. Guiomar de Ulloa and Father Ibáñez keep working while the prohibition of the confessor of Mother Teresa remains in force, and while she is absent from Avila. They write to Rome asking for the necessary permissions, and thanks to their collaboration, when Mother Teresa returns to Avila, they are able to give her a Brief from the Pope authorising the foundation.

CHAPTER VII

THE LITTLE CONVENT
OF SAINT JOSEPH

It's the 24th of August, 1562. The town neighbours of the eastern suburb of Avila, who are sleeping quietly in the houses outside the city walls, are awoken with surprise by the happy swinging of the little bell, that sounds throughout the area. It is a joyous sound, that announces good news. When the most curious go looking for the place in which the mysterious little bell is ringing, they find a humble little house: low stone walls, narrow and grilled windows, shadowy corridors, low ceilings of dark wood. Next to the house, there is a tiny chapel and a small garden with almond trees. The little bell is swinging next to the door. It announces the inauguration of the little convent of Mother Teresa.

It is a simple ceremony, but full of emotion. At the chapel altar, Father Daza, a theologian cleric, celebrates the inaugural Mass. There are various people taking part: Father Julian de Avila, who is to be the chaplain of the new convent; Gonzalo de Aranda and Francisco de Salcedo, friends of Mother Teresa; two nuns from the Incarnation, and Mrs. Juana de Ahumada with her husband Mr. Juan de Ovalle.

Next to the lectern, behind a wooden grill, four young ladies on their knees can be distinguished next to Mother. They are awaiting the holy Discalced habit, as they are to be the first to wear it before the world. They are dressed in white, their

THE SMALL BROKEN BELL. On the 24th of August, 1562, at sunrise, this "small bell that weighs three pounds or a little more, that had come out of the casting with a fairly big hole", announced to the city of Avila the inauguration of the first Teresian foundation.

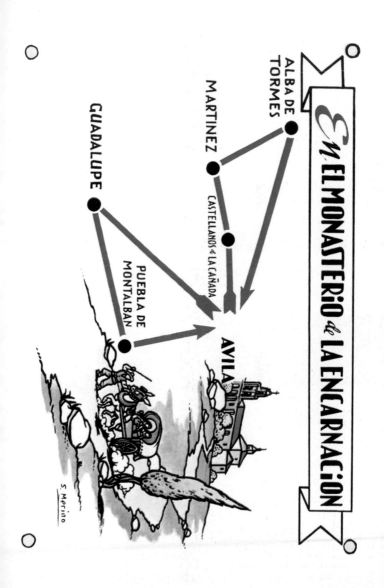

En EL MONASTERiO de LA ENCARNACiÓN

ALBA DE TORMES

MARTINEZ

CASTELLANOS de LA CAÑADA

GUADALUPE

PUEBLA DE MONTALBAN

AVILA

S. Merino

On the 2nd of November of 1535, with twenty years of age, Teresa goes through this door that leads to the cloister of Carmel. It took her three years to convince herself that it was "the best and most sure state of life" (*Life* 3, 5).

"I remember that when I left my father's home, I felt that separation so keenly that the feeling will not be greater, I think, when I die" (*Life* 4, 1).

THE MONASTERY OF THE INCARNATION OF AVILA.

17. The cloister with its cells.

18. The refectory.

19. The parlour. It was here where she spoke to Saint Francis of Borja and Saint Peter of Alcántara.

20. Small kitchen used by the saint.

21

22

24. **ECCE HOMO.**

"My soul was quite tired... One day, while entering into the oratory, I saw an image... It was of Christ, who appears in it terribly injured, and so devout, that in looking at it, I was utterly distressed to see Him like that... I threw myself next to Him, shedding many tears, pleading Him to strengthen me once and for all, so that I may not offend Him ever again..." (*Life* 9, 1).

25. **ALDEA DEL PALO (Zamora). House and property of Mrs. Guiomar de Ulloa, which later on would be converted into a convent of Alcanterine Franciscans. She stayed here for four months in company of her friend Mrs. Guiomar, taking care of Father Prádanos. Today, only ruins are left.**

27. **THE ENTRANCE TO THE PALACE OF MRS. GUIOMAR, IN AVILA.**

28. **AVILA. Mosén Rubín.**

29. **TOLEDO. Saint Peter Martyr.**

30. SAINT VINCENT. Our Lady of Soterraña.

31. Façade of the convent.

SAINT JOSEPH OF AVILA:

It was here, on the 24th of August of 1562, where Mother Teresa started her foundational adventure. In a poor house and with only four nuns, one of the most fecund and most original spiritual movements of the history of the Church was born. Teresa was thinking of the stable in Bethlehem; we think of the mustard seed.

32.   Hermitage in the garden of the convent.

"...the house seemed very small to me, and so much so, that it didn't seem like a monastery at all... I went to the house and started drawing up plans, and I found, even though it was very small, that it had everything necessary for a monastery... everything rough and unpolished, but sufficient enough so that it wouldn't be harmful to health..." (*Life* 33, 12).

This room reflects that poverty and smallness of the primitive convent. Here, Saint Teresa exercised herself as a cook, as all of her nuns do.

33. **The primitive kitchen of Saint Joseph of Avila.**

34. **THE UPPER CORREDOR OF THE CENTRAL PATIO.** The broken bell
that announced the inauguration of this first Teresian Carmel can be
seen hanging from the ceiling.

35.   **ROADS for a "traveller". In the year 1567 Father Rubeo, the General
of the Order, reaches Avila, and visits the small convent of Saint
Joseph. "With the desire that this beginning may flourish and extend,
he gave me very extensive patents to found more monasteries... Then
everything seemed very possible to me, and I put myself to work to
make it a reality"** (*Foundations* 2, 3.6).

hands united, eyes looking down and face shining with a sweet virginal expression. They look
like angels.

Once Mass has finished, the ceremony of the
taking of the habit takes place. Mother puts the
rough cloth, the wimple, the white cape, and the
veil on each of the novices. And all of this is being
accompanied by prayers and liturgical blessings
that Father Daza recites from the altar, while looking towards the choir grill. When the foundress
sees before her the four nuns with their discalced
feet and white cape, she feels so profoundly over-
whelmed that she can't help showing her emotion.
Her eyes are glowing with enthusiasm, and a sweet
and maternal smile opens on her lips. In the atmosphere of the chapel which is fragranced with
incense, a spirit of purity floats around in a way
that makes one bring to mind the stable in Bethlehem. The grand work of the Reform of Carmel has
begun. The little bell still swings happily, next to
the entrance, as a proclamation of the divine enterprise undertaken by Mother.

From that moment, Avila starts to live centred
around the small convent of Saint Joseph, as its
foundress wanted to call it. The entire city feels
affected by the announcement of the inauguration
of the convent. Chief magistrate and governors,
nobles and workers, clerics and lay people move
into action and take part in the matter, as though
the life of the whole dominion depended on it.
Many years had gone by, more than a century,
since the last time the city had felt so affected.

It had been in the year 1465. In the extremities of the city, a platform had been erected in the form of a throne. A statue of James IV was left seated on it, dressed in black and in his royal garments: crown, sceptre, sword, collars... The multitude extends before him on the plain. The figure of the King can be seen from every angle. The town crier throws terrible accusations against James IV, while the people listen in absolute silence, their nerves tense with emotion, as they shout and curse impatiently. After the reading of the declaration is made, the Archbishop of Toledo climbs the throne and takes away the royal crown from the head of the statue. The Count of Benavente approaches and he removes the sceptre. Then the Count of Plascencia goes and unstraps the sword. Right after him, Mr. Diego López of Zúñiga takes the statue and throws it to the ground, while vigorous arms lift high a small boy, Prince Alfonso, and the nobles shout ardently: "Castille for King Alfonso!" The drums and trumpets sound, and the crowd acclaims the new King, who receives the oath of fidelity of the nobles, prelates and people, who kiss his hands while passing by. Avila lived with intense emotion the days of his event that seemed to change the course of Spanish history.

Now too, there is a coming and going of governors, nobles and workers. Even friars and clerics

FAÇADE OF SAINT JOSEPH. The first foundation of Saint Teresa and the birthplace of her Reform.

intervene excitedly, as though it were a vital question for Avila. Everyone has something to say about the enterprise of Mother Teresa. Those who had condemned it when it was only a project are now furious now that they see it made reality. Those who had looked upon it indifferently or had approved of it, are shocked because of the commotion that it has produced in the society of Avila. A certain feeling in the air announces frightful happenings.

One morning, while the discalced nuns are working on the spinning wheel and making embroidery, some heavy door knocks are heard in the poor small convent. When they answer, they hear voices outside demanding them to abandon the convent. It is the Chief Magistrate Carvajal, who threatens to break the door down if they don't come out straight away, because the Council has decided to dissolve the foundation. But the four little nuns respond that they won't leave the cloister unless Mother Teresa tells them to do so, because she was the one who let them enter there.

The Magistrate returns furious to the Council. New deliberations. Some advise that they should consult with all the most significant people of the city, because this matter is too important for the Council to resolve alone, and so they determine that they will convoke a general meeting, so that it may decide. To this meeting representatives of the Church, of the Religious Orders, of the clergy, of the nobles and of the different trades of the city

will be summoned. It will be the only way to resolve
this affair that everybody is so interested in.

* * *

The 30th of August. It is Sunday. At three
o'clock in the afternoon, while the youth go walking below the arcade of the square, the bell of the
Council rings, calling all to the extraordinary
meeting. A little while after, the important per-
sonalities begin to arrive, crossing the square
before the curiosity of the people, and they enter
into the Municipal building. From one side, the
Magistrate and the governors, the notaries and
the bailiffs enter; on the other, the Dean, a canon,
the Precentor of the Cathedral and the Provost of
the Bishopric. With their white and black habit,
the Dominican Father Pedro Serrano, prior of St.
Tomas', accompanied by the theologian Father
Domingo Báñez; the Guardian of the Franciscans, Father Martín de Aguilera, and Father Her-
nando de Valderrábano, preacher of the same
Order, are also seen. From further away, the Pre-
monstratensian Abbot of the Convent of Sancti
Spiritus, all dressed in white; the Benedictine
Abbot of Our Lady of the Antigua, with his large
black habit; the Jesuits Ripalda and Baltasar
Álvarez; the graduated Daza, Cimbrón and Orte-
ga, and the nobles Cristóbal Juárez and Alonso
de Robledo are also coming. All of them cross the
town square and enter into the City Council
Building. The townsfolk, who are aware of the

objectives of the assembly, await in the square
the conclusions of the meeting.

What is going on inside? The Chief Magistrate
presents the well known case: it has to do with
the demolition or the permanency of the Convent
of Saint Joseph, founded six days ago by Mother
Teresa. The Provost of the Bishopric stands up
and reads, on behalf of the Bishop, the Pontifical
Brief which authorises the foundation, and with-
draws from the meeting room. The opinions and
discussions start straight away. Almost everyone
is against the idea. Clergy, friars, abbots and theologians, graduates and nobleman think that the
new foundation is a threat to the rest of the
Monasteries, and the Pontifical Brief need not be
executed, as not all of the conditions described in
it have been met. It is necessary, therefore, to can-
cel the foundation, to eliminate the Convent. And
the quicker, the better.

Almost all sit down. The Jesuits, are silent, they
don't either approve or condemn. When there is
silence in the chamber, the Dominican Friar,
Father Domingo Báñez stands up, ready to talk.
Everyone turns to look at the young theologian
with the white and black habit. His voice
resounds with seriousness and with strength.
And he speaks with courage. It is necessary to
reflect on the matter, he says. Such an important
matter, as is the case of the suppression of the
Convent of Saint Joseph, cannot be decided light-
ly. There is a Brief from the Pope and an author-
ization from the Bishop that favour it. It is also a

deed for the glory of God, and Mother Teresa, who has a good spirit, puts into it the best of desires for the salvation and sanctification of souls. Let us leave the matter in the hands of the Bishop —he finishes saying— because, being an ecclesiastical matter as it is, it is he, more than the City Council, who is the competent authority to resolve it.

When Father Domingo Báñez sits down, his words linger in the atmosphere of the room as a warning from heaven. The members of the assembly look at each other in a silence of indecision. Mother Teresa's defender has triumphed. His reasons have calmed spirits down, and when the Chief Magistrate speaks this time, it is to propose, interpreting the effect that the words of Father Báñez had provoked in all, that the Lord Bishop be informed once again before making a final decision on the fate of the Discalced Convent.

This is how the solemn Consistory finished on that Sunday afternoon of August. The people who were waiting outside, look curiously and chatter while the distinguished men, that have assisted the meeting, leave to disperse themselves in different directions. The Dominicans go eastward, to go down the Amblés Valley; the Franciscans toward the north, in search of their Convent of Saint Francis outside the city walls... Meanwhile, excited groups of people stay in the town square, commenting on the outcome of the Consistory.

CHAPTER VIII

THE LIFE OF THE DISCALCED NUNS

Mother Teresa is finally with her daughters in Saint Joseph's. She has suffered a lot to get there. On the very day of the foundation, they obliged her to leave her little convent and to enclose herself in the convent she came from: the Incarnation. From there she did whatever she could: she encouraged her Discalced nuns, who were being persecuted; she defended the foundation against the Council that had presented a lawsuit to the King; she persevered firm in her resolutions against the whole city and she had responded to all the accusations, from high and low, that they had thrown at her for her insistence in maintaining the foundation.

But one day in August, exactly a year after the inauguration of the convent, the people of Avila notice how Mother Teresa climbs the hill on the

CARMELITES IN RECREATION.

north of the city, she enters into the basilica of Saint Vincent, she leaves it, this time discalced, and she walks, next the city walls, to the little convent of Saint Joseph. Her eyes are glowing with joy and in her stride she carries a certain air of triumphant decision. The little bell of the turn, rings like never before, as though it had recognised the hand of the foundress who calls, and when the door opens, the four novices throw themselves into the arms of their Mother. With her, an assurance and joy enters into the convent of Saint Joseph, never known since the day of the foundation. The young novices, who had felt orphaned for a time now, are comforted with maternal warmth once again. Even the cloisters, cells and work rooms seem more joyful with the presence of the holy Mother.

* * *

And what a life they live, so recollected, Mother and her nuns! At 5 o'clock in the morning, the sound of the little bell fills the silent cloister. It calls the nuns to prayer. The doors of their cells open softly, and the nuns start to come out, gliding like shadows along the cloister which is dimly lit by a small candle. They enter into the choir and kneel down next to the grill that looks out into the chapel. A community invocation of the Holy Spirit; one of the nuns reads a passage from some spiritual book to help their meditation, and then absolute silence that will last an hour. They are in mental prayer. They think about God, about the mysteries of Christ, about human misery. And they pray: they pray for the Church, for priests, for the Lutherans who are increasing in number in Germany, France and Flanders, and that are threatening to enter into Spain. Mother continually reminds them that these are to be the objectives and the aims of their prayer. This is why she and God had brought them together.

REFECTORY. The photograph was taken in the convent of Valladolid, that conserves the floor and the tables exactly how they were in the times of the foundation.

After mental prayer, they pray a part of the Divine Office. The sweet nun's voices resound as voices of angels in the choir, coming out from the grilled windows and slipping down the solitary and silent streets. Afterward, comes the Mass, communion, ordering of the cells, and work in their different jobs. Sometimes, the coming and going of the nuns through the work areas and corridors gives to the small convent the impression of being like a silent, but hardworking beehive.

On top of the seat of the Mother in the refectory, a wooden cross is presiding, and on the table, there is a skull. Small tables made of rough wood, without carvings or any paint; small jars and bowls made of baked clay; cutlery also made of wood: this is what constitutes their dinning suite. They gather together here to eat the herbs picked from the garden and some cucumbers or some leaves from the grape vine, seasoned with a few drops of oil. On feast days, there is something special: an egg for each nun. Many times, Mother Teresa fries them herself. The nuns have even seen her in ecstasy while holding in her hand the frying pan, and other times she would repeat to them smilingly: "Daughters, God dwells among the pots and pans!"

And how happy they are all in their poverty, their abstinence and the rigorous fast they undergo during more that seven months in the year!

*   *   *

When they leave the refectory —while praying psalms and petitions— they go toward the small garden if there is good weather, or to a small room if it's cold or raining. It is the hour of recreation. The Mother Foundress gives as much importance to this part of the horarium as to the other most holy and spiritual of exercises. An honourable rest is also necessary in human life. The arc cannot always be tensed without eventually breaking, and the tension of an austere life could otherwise lead to health and even spiritual problems.

And how pleasant is that recreation time in the convent of Saint Joseph! They talk, they sing, they laugh, they work. The nuns, seated on the floor, sow and embroider, they prepare scapulars, repair altar cloths or paint a small curtain for the Tabernacle. Mother Teresa, seated with them, talks and gives life to the recreation, while her hands turn the spindle and the distaff.

On feast days, instead of working, they sing alleluias composed by the saint. At Christmas they play different kinds of drums, the castanets, blow whistles, and they even dance around the nativity of the Child Jesus recently born.

They have many happy and holy times together, animated by the Mother Reformer. One day, the nuns find themselves quite annoyed because of some untimely little animals that start to grow in their woollen tunics. They'll have to ask God to free them of this pest. Mother organises a rogation before a statue they have of Jesus Christ in the choir. But they will not go there reciting

psalms or litanies: they will sing some spiritual poems that the saint has composed for the occasion. On that day, in the evening, when the twilight hardly enlightens the narrow cloisters, the low ceiling, or the brick floors, the nuns head towards the choir in two rows. Mother presides, and they sing, alternating:

ALL: *Now, that you give us new clothing*
Oh Heavenly King,
Free from the creepy foes
These woollen clothes.

MOTHER: Daughters, who have embraced
the cross, Prepare to fight.
And to Jesus, who is your light,
Ask his favour.
He will be your heavenly knight,
Before the danger.

ALL: *Free from the creepy foes*
These woollen clothes.

MOTHER: Disturbing is this nasty mob
In our petitions,
The spirit is not centred
In our devotions;
Without regard, keep the heart in God
Most strengthened.

CASTANETS. The saint wanted for all her convents an atmosphere of sincere joy and she was the first to contribute with Christmas songs and verses on the festivities of Christmas and for the professions of the nuns. These castanets were used by the saint and are conserved in the convent of the Discalced Carmelite nuns in Palencia.

ALL: *Free from the creepy foes*
                These woollen clothes.
MOTHER: Since you've come here to die
                  Never loose heart,
                And of such a bad company
                  Never take fright
                In God you'll find the remedy
                  To your cry.
ALL: *Now, that you give us new clothing*
                Oh Heavenly King,
                Free from the creepy foes
                These woollen clothes

And the miracle works. The nuns are never again to feel troubled by the untimely little animals, and from then on, that statue of Jesus will be called "The Christ of the Flees".

*   *   *

With what devotion the Discalced nuns return to their practices of piety and penance after those times of spiritual amusement! The holy joy prolongs in the soul during all of the cloistered activities. We could say that the smile that the Mother Foundress provokes in recreation time doesn't disappear from the lips of her daughters in any of their regular exercises. In this way, she manages to give to her spirituality a jovial character that is typical of Saint Teresa, that dispels from the cloisters that melancholic, withdrawn, frowning and gloomy kind of sanctity, that Mother

detested as a terrible spiritual sickness, as though it were a contagious pest or an incurable bad habit.

That is why everything they do is kept in a simple and joyful atmosphere: the penances, the choral exercises, the manual work...

In the afternoon, at three o'clock, after praying Vespers, there is absolute silence in Saint Joseph's. Neither the noise of doors, nor the footsteps of nuns, not even the sweet eco of the recitation of psalms in the choir can be heard. It's because each nun is recollected in her cell, doing her manual work. Modestly seated on the floor, on the bed, or on a square piece of cork that preserves from humidity, they work on their task. While with their hands they sew, embroider or weave hemp for the soles of their poor sandals, their thoughts fly like a butterfly attracted by the rooms of the Mystical Castle in search of the Beloved.

At five o'clock, they pray Compline; and straight after, in the refectory with its bare wooden cross and skull, they have a simple supper: a glass of water, and some vegetables or some salad in the bowl of baked clay. At eight o'clock, they have another hour of mental prayer, and the paused and feverous recitation of Matins. Afterward comes the examination of conscience, the discipline and petitions. They recollect themselves in their cells once again to dedicate themselves to their devotions until they receive the signal to retire. It's an impressive signal: at eleven o'clock, nine rhythmic knocks coming from little wooden blocks and given by one of the nuns while kneeling down at one end of the corridor are heard throughout the cloister: Clack, clack, clack; clack, clack, clack; clack, clack, clack! All the nuns open the doors of their respective cells and kneel down at the entrance. Then the voice of the nun with the wooden blocks is heard reciting some semitoned verses on death, on glory, or on the excellence of one of the virtues:

> You'll die only once
> And in an uncertain circumstance
> If you choose the wrong door
> The consequence will be forever more...

And while the little arrow embeds in the thought of the nuns, Mother passes by giving a blessing to each of them. They are now allowed to sleep on their bed of a wooden board, on the hard and narrow straw mattress, and slip into their course woollen sheets. Until the next day in which the little bell rings again, calling them to prayer.

CHAPTER IX

THE FIRST ADVENTURES AS
A FOUNDRESS

Along the road from Avila to Arévalo, three awning covered wagons lift clouds of dust. The sun, that is in its summit, has dried up the grass and has tanned the fields and sideways. The air seems to burn. The donkeys are lazily pulling the wooden wagons, that screech and swerve along the rough and rocky road. On the sides, there are some young people walking on foot, and a priest on a horse. Inside, underneath the wagon's awning, heated by the sun, there are some nuns, uncomfortably seated among the rudimentary household items, praying psalms and singing spiritual songs. They are Mother Teresa and seven nuns. They are travelling with the enthusiasm of being foundresses. It is the 12th of August 1567.

While they go by the little villages, the "august men" —wide straw hats, bare and tanned arms, faces darkened by the sun— stop to gaze at the mysterious caravan that slowly passes by. They go past small bare hills, fields with sheaves of recently reaped wheat, sown moors of rocks and dry thistles, old streams of dry and cracked mud, half cooked by the strength of the sun.

At dusk, they distinguish at a distance, the parapets of the castle and the towers of the churches of Arévalo, all illuminated by the fire coloured sunset. They are surrounded by a green band: poplars that grow on the bank of the River Adaja, whose waters, quite diminished, filter through the sand. And there, in the noble and pacific Castillian village, which not long ago had been the childhood residence of Queen Elizabeth, Mother Teresa and her escort stay the night.

The next day, they resume their journey. But they no longer travel in awning covered wagons. That would attract too much attention. It is necessary to enter into Medina silently, because some difficulties have arisen, and the noise could hinder the foundation. So she dismisses the stable boys who had come to help, so they can return to Avila with the wagons; she leaves four nuns in a close by village, and with her, two other nuns and Julian de Avila mount on some mules and the set

THE CHRIST OF THE FOUNDATIONS. This image of Christ presided the "travelling cloister" of the Teresian carriages. It is conserved in the Natal House of the saint in Avila.

out for Medina. Mother Teresa rides well. She
has certain ability to ride and control the small
mule when it frightens or loses control.

It's a long road. Night is falling, and they still
can't make out in the distance the majestic shadow of the grand castle of Medina, or the tower of
the collegiate church. But it doesn't matter. Mother prefers to enter Medina during the night, when
nobody will be able to see them. It's ten o'clock,
eleven o'clock, and the Chaplain and foundress-

**SADDLE. Very deteriorated. It was used by Saint Teresa
in one of her journeys from Medina to Avila. It is conserved
in the primitive convent of Saint Joseph.**

es are still travelling along the narrow and winding dirt track. The stars are shining like diamonds in the clear sky, and the land still reflects the heat that the August Castillian sun has beamed down during the day.

It's twelve o'clock when they reach the town, twelve o'clock at night on the eve of the festivity of the Assumption of Our Lady. They look for the most abandoned outskirts, and the most silent alleys to enter the city and reach the Carmelite Convent. Julian de Avila knocks at the door, knocks which resound in the silence of the tranquil night, reflecting an eco, which seems to hit the high and thick walls of the castle far away. Some people begin to move around. An uproar of a group approaches. Mother wants to hurry on; she is afraid that they may find them. They gather the few belongings that they have prepared in Carmel to say Mass, and they head towards the small house which is to be their convent.

But it's too late. The uproar is now quite close. The running footsteps of people and the heavy trot of cattle are heard. The encounter is unavoidable. Mother, the nuns, Julian de Avila, a Chaplain of the Bishop and three or four Carmelite friars that have come to accompany them from the Carmelite Convent, are all walking briskly along the street. Each one with their luggage: altar cloths, chalice, missal, cruets... They go stealthily, as though they had been robbing something and were escaping from the police. Behind them, the bulls that they are going to be used for the

CONVENT OF MEDINA DEL CAMPO. Primitive balcony.

next day's festivity are closing in rapidly. When
the crowd meets up with Mother, the nuns, the
priests and friars, cheeky comments, laughter
and whistles are heard. But nor Mother, nor any
of those who accompany her react in any way:
they keep silence and keep walking.

In the early morning, at daybreak, after a few
hours occupied in making a chapel in the

entrance of the house, which is to be transformed into a convent, Mother Teresa and her nuns hear Mass. The second foundation has been inaugurated. The holy Reformer weeps for joy as she prostrates before the Holy Sacrament.

* * *

Several days have past. In the parlour of the recently founded convent, Mother Teresa and a young, small friar are in conversation. The name of the friar is Father John. He has come from Salamanca, where he is completing his university studies, and has recently celebrated his first Mass. The Mother Foundress, who has called for him, explains to him her projects: she wants to start the Reform in the friars, a Reform identical to that which she is undertaking in the nuns. And she is looking for suitable subjects for the task. She has already spoken to the Prior of Medina, who has offered himself enthusiastically. But he is old. And she wants this to be gleaming with the brightness of youth, without the ailments or lingerings of the mitigated way of life, because the austerity and recollection that are to be the foundation of the Reform, call for it. "Maybe", the saint suggests, "with your fresh theological formation, with the desires that they tell me you have for a penitent and recollected life, in the plenitude of your youth... Wouldn't you like to be the foundation stone of this new project?"

DOMINE

P. Fr Ioannes a Cruce

ANTHONY OF JESUS AND SAINT JOHN OF THE CROSS.
The author of these portraits of the first two Discalced
Carmelites is unknown. It is dated towards the end of the
seventeenth century. They are conserved in the convent of
the Carmelite Fathers in Segovia.

The words of this nun have the accent and the persuasion of a heavenly voice. Father John smiles and offers a condition: he agrees only if he doesn't have to wait very long to begin. He feels certain urgency. He had already decided to be a Carthusian monk as soon as he finished his studies in Salamanca. And he doesn't want to delay his change of life. If then, everything is ready to start the Reform... Mother assures him of this, and the little saint, Father John, promises to be the first Discalced Carmelite. Saint Teresa feels deeply moved: her eyes sparkle, her heart throbs within her chest. When Father John bids farewell and leaves the parlour, Mother runs excitedly to give the good news to her nuns, who are in recreation: "Daughters", she announces, "blessed be God, as I now have one and a half friars for the foundation of the Discalced Carmelites".

*   *   *

Father John has undergone his last year of studies in the University of Salamanca. Mother Teresa, meanwhile, has been in Alcalá, in Toledo, in Malagón, and in Avila. She has consolidated

---

DURUELO. This is Duruelo: a small and solitary town, lost among oak trees, on the boundary between Avila and Salamanca. It was here, on the 28th of November, 1568, where Saint John of the Cross inaugurated the first foundation of Discalced Carmelite friars. It marks the extension of the Teresian Reform to the masculine branch of the Order.

her third foundation in the Manchegan village, and she has seen in Duruelo, the sweet little corner of the province of Avila, a small house that someone has offered her to be the first monastery of friars. Towards the end of June, she returns to Medina, where she awaits Father John, after having finished his studies in Salamanca.

When they meet in the poor parlour of the Discalced nuns, Mother shows him the plan of the future monastery of Duruelo: an entrance, two bedrooms, a small kitchen and an attic. The young and small Carmelite smiles. "It is still very big for me", he says, looking at Mother, who smiles as well.

A few minutes later, the scene changes. On the inside of the grill, Mother Teresa, surrounded by her nuns. On the outside of the grill, Father John, with his austere, short and narrow habit, with his bare feet and happy expression, offers, while standing in the middle of the parlour, the sweet and humble image of the first Discalced Carmelite. The habit he is wearing has been sowed by Mother Teresa and her nuns. The Mother becomes absorbed while contemplating the final result. Her dream of a reform among the friars is now a reality. And that little saint, Father John, with soul and talent of a giant in such a small body, is the maximum guarantee of success for the project she has so many times dreamt of.

And the distinguished reformer isn't wrong. Before the end of the year, once the foundation of Valladolid has been realised, and she is on her way to Toledo, the saint can contemplate the small convent of Father John in a pleasant corner of Castille. Mother is astonished: a tiny and poor but clean chapel, with an abundance of crosses and skulls; two small cells where the friars don't fit unless they kneel or lie down; they use straw found on the floor as beds, with a stone as a pillow. On the roof the tiles are broken in a way which allows the snow to fall on top of them while they are praying at midnight. And Father John smiles in the midst of that austere and mortifying solitude. Wasn't this the ideal she had dreamt of as a Foundress?

When she leaves and continues her journey, she carries with her the sweet memory of that little monastery, small like a cradle, where the Discalced Reform, under the sun and the pure and clear air of Castille, is being formed.

SAINT TERESA LOSES THE WAY AND IS GUIDED BY ANGELES.

CHAPTER X

FOUNDING AND GOVERNING

The Jewish Suburb of Toledo. Narrow, dead ended and winding streets around the Moorish style synagogue, full of Hebrew and Arabic inscriptions, that stand out because of the light that enters through the arched windows in the brick walls. At the bottom of the city, on the western side, the curving Tajo River, that farewells Toledo to run into the plains towards Extremadura. Further away, on the other side of the river, the typical view of the fields with their white houses, its prickly pears, its apricot and olive trees.

There, close to the synagogue, in a small, low and narrow house with a small patio, Mother Teresa has just inaugurated her fifth foundation. At night, while the city sleeps silently, the constant sound of the waters that flow into the Tajo River enters through the small narrow windows of the chapel, and it mixes with the recitation of

FAÇADE OF THE CARMEL OF TOLEDO.

psalms and with the loving sighs of the nuns in prayer. The holy Reformer is thrilled. They don't have anything to eat, but the atmosphere is admirable, and Jesus has yet another Tabernacle in the heights of the imperial city.

However, she will not be able to enjoy the small house for very long. Having just inaugurated the foundation, while Mother and her nuns are eating a humble stew in the refectory, a knocking of the door is heard. It is a servant of the Princess of Eboli. He has brought a letter, a carriage and instructions to take Mother Teresa to Pastrana. The Princess calls her to go there, to meet her so that she can inspect the convent she has prepared next to the Palace for a new foundation of Discalced nuns. The saint vacillates somewhat, as she is worried about leaving the foundation in Toledo, still making its first steps, but her confessor advises her that she should make the journey, and so the foundress sets out to the village of the Princess.

* * *

Everything has been arranged in Pastrana: in the Palace of the Princess they have large rooms reserved for her and her nuns while they organise the house that is to be the monastery; the service of the maids that attend to all the needs of the Discalced nuns; the careful attention of the Princess who tries to spoil the nuns. But there is something that is going to make her stay there quite unpleasant: certain demands and fancies of the Princess, who wants to intervene in the intimacy of the life of the nuns. And the saint considers this untouchable. She will not make concessions in this. Not the title, not the money, not the social influence, not even the favours received give the right to the wife of Prince Ruy Gómez to change the spirit and the way of life of the Discalced nuns. The Mother Foundress lets them know her thought on this, and she is prepared to abandon the Palace and the foundation before giving in on this, as she considers it a kind of profanation.

PASTRANA. The Palace of the Princess of Eboli.

There is heated discussion in the highly decorated halls of the Palace; there are threats from
the Princess, who believes she has been offend-
ed; there are insinuations on behalf of the saint,
that she will return to Madrid without having
inaugurated the convent. They are fancies and
passing whims of the lady who is thwarted before
the holy and firm strength of Mother. At last the
Prince manages to deviate the demands of his
wife, and the foundation is realised. But nobody
is entirely happy: the Princess, because it hasn't
been done according to her fancy; the saint,
because she sees in the Princess, who keeps want-
ing to intervene in what she shouldn't, a danger
for the peace of her religious nuns.

With this bitter premonition, Saint Teresa leaves
Pastrana. When she crosses mountains and river
streams on her way to Madrid and Toledo, while
her face is being gratified by the tepid air full of
the essence of the wild flowers of the area that
flower at this time of year, she feels a kind of wound
in her soul made by her profound concern for the
outcome of those angels, her daughters that she
has left behind, almost at the mercy of the incon-
sistent, determined and resentful Princess.

*   *   *

Four months have passed. It is the night of All
Souls of 1570 in Salamanca. There is a mournful
atmosphere in the city. The sad clamour of the
bells of the one hundred churches and convents

sounds like a long and immense moan of the souls
whose shadows seem to linger around the bell towers. In an old house, left in bad conditions, towards
the north of the city, two nuns are bolting up doors
and windows that don't quite fit too well in their
frames. They are Mother Teresa and Maria of the
Sacrament, her companion, recently arrived from
Avila, after having undergone a cold and rainy
journey. They have come to begin another foundation. Some moments before, that old house was
full of the hustle and bustle of university students,
who refused to leave the building to the Discalced
nun. But the house, with its big rooms, long and
dark corridors, large attic, has now been left in
absolute silence. Through the cracks of the windows the funeral clamour of the bells and the whis-
tle of the wind also seem to moan.

Mother Teresa's companion is afraid: she is
afraid of the students, as she thinks that maybe
they are still hiding in some corner of the building, she is afraid of the dead, that moan from the
heights of the bell towers. The saint laughs at the
fears of the sister, who looks from one side to the
other, scared stiff, as though she were about to
find some untouchable shadows slowly entering
without having to open the door.

Eventually, exhausted with fatigue and lack of
sleep, they lie down on some straw they have
found and they cover themselves with some poor
blankets they have lent to them. Maria of the
Sacrament is still afraid. She thinks of the dead,
and she lifts up her head nervously every time she

hears the wooden windows creaking. "What are you looking at?" asks Mother, "Don't you see that no one can enter?" "Mother", she replies, "I was just thinking… if I was to die tonight, what would you do here, on your own?" "Sister, if that comes to happen, then I will think what I will have to do. For now, please let me sleep". And a few minutes later, the two nuns, exhausted from the day's work, sleep on a hump of straw, having wrapped themselves up in two borrowed blankets.

In the morning, when all the shadows and fears have passed by, they prepare a small altar with some wooden planks; they clean the corridors, rooms and stair cases that the students hadn't left so clean, and the first Mass is celebrated. The foundation has been inaugurated. The holy Reformer is happy in the house and later comments with humour, the noises, the winds and the fears of her sister that night of the souls.

*   *   *

A few days later, the students, who are noisily talking near the entrance of the University while they wait for classes to begin, see two nuns walk past them with their white capes and black veils. The loud talking is converted into silence. The students look with curiosity. "It's her", they say in a low voice, "Mother Teresa, the one that on the night of the souls threw us out of the house to convert it into a convent". And they follow her with their eyes until they lose sight of her as she

THE PATIO OF THE INCARNATION. Engraving of the
nineteenth century.

enters the alleys near the Cathedral, among the shadows of the Gallo Tower.

The saint goes down towards the River Tormes and crosses it on the Roman bridge and takes the imperial road that leads to Alba de Tormes. The Dukes have called for her so that she may found a convent in their town, and away she goes, the distinguished reformer, among the ploughed fields and oak trees. When she enters into the Duke's Palace, while her sandals sink into the thick carpet, her eyes are dazzled by the shining jewels and precious armoury that cover the walls and fill the gold decorated furniture. She speaks with the Dukes; draws up contracts with the accountants for the foundation; she writes up the property deeds with the notary; she directs the repairs needed in the houses that are to form the convent, and on the 25th of January, 1571, the monastery is inaugurated. It is to be here, with time, next to the River Tormes, where the sepulchre and reliquary of the incorrupt body and the transverberated heart of the sublime Reformer will come to rest.

* * *

While Mother travels around Castille in this manner, founding convents of observance and recollection, the convent of the Incarnation in Avila is threatened with being materially and spiritually ruined. The nuns, who are quite fond of the parlour, are not so worried about the life of spiritual perfection, and there is such a state of confusion that even the economic side of things is being neglected. They come to lack even the most necessary sustenance. The superiors take note of the danger, and they think that Mother Teresa would be the only one capable of containing so much decadence. She, full of wit, integrity and gentleness, once she is named Prioress, will be able to do the miracle.

And on the 6th of October the doors of the convent are opened to receive the new superior. But the nuns are not happy about it. There are suspicious looks, distrustful comments, and even protests manifested in words and attitudes. They think that Mother is going to oblige them to subjugate themselves to the rigour of her Reform; that she will try to make them Discalced by force, and they are ready to oppose themselves to this, using all the means they have at reach.

The Provincial, that accompanies Mother Teresa for her entrance, demands that they reunite themselves for a Chapter meeting. Once the nuns are together, who can't hide their nervousness, the Provincial reads with a serious tone of voice, the license whereby the Apostolic Visitor names Mother Teresa the Prioress of the Incarnation. He hasn't finished reading, when a clamour of protests and even insults to the saint drowns the last words of the Superior. Mother, who is standing next to the seat of the Provincial, calmly puts up with the uproar of the nuns. Once they manage to achieve silence, the Provincial asks the nuns: "Don't you want Mother Teresa of Jesus?". There is a moment of indecision.

Nobody answers. Finally, one of them, Catherine of Castro, stands up and says: "We want her and we love her". And the question is settled. The majority of the nuns make these words their own, and the saint is admitted as Prioress of the Incarnation.

The next day, Mother convokes a Conventual Chapter in the choir. Some go with fear; others with distrust; and the rest of them in an attitude of expectancy. Against the traditional custom, Mother Teresa doesn't sit in the Prioress' seat. She has put there a statue of Our Lady, and in her hands she has put the keys of the convent, and she sits at the foot of the statue. There is absolute silence. The nuns contain even their breath in expectation of the first words she is to pronounce. And then the sweet and loving voice of the holy Prioress is heard:

"Ladies, Mothers and Sisters of mine: Our Lord, by means of obedience, has sent me to this house, to carry out this office... I have only come to serve you and to comfort you in everything I can. I am a daughter of this house, and a sister of you all. Do not fear my government, because, even though until now I have lived and governed Discalced nuns, I know well, thanks to the goodness of God, how to govern those who are not Discalced..."

They have been won over. The words of Mother are received as words of comfort and light for the spirits of the nuns. All the suspicions are dissipated. From that moment, all will see in her a solicitous and loving Mother that worries about the welfare of her daughters. And a few months later, the convent and community that had been in such a bad state, under the care of Saint Teresa and the spiritual direction of Saint John of the Cross, who comes, called by her, as the confessor of the nuns, will be a model of observance, recollection and spiritual prosperity.

CHAPTER XI

ON THE BANKS OF THE RIVER GUADALQUIVIR

The foundational work of Mother Teresa extends. She has travelled across Castille and the "Mancha": Avila, Medina del Campo, Malagón, Valladolid, Toledo, Pastrana, Salamanca, Alba de Tormes... Rest and tranquillity are not on her plans. She has just founded the convent of Segovia, and they are already awaiting her in lands bathed by the river Guadalquivir. And there goes the Mother, while letting the gleaming sun of Andalucía shine down on her white cape.

She first arrives to Beas, a beautiful but small village which lies in the valley of a mountain where orange, pomegranate and lemon trees grow all around. It is no longer cold. The smell of the perfume of the almond tree flowers flood the atmosphere, and the muttering of the water that jumps between fig and olive trees is perceived. It

FATHER GRACIÁN. Tiny portrait which is conserved in the Carmelite convent in Consuegra. "He is complete in my eyes, and for us he is better that we could even think to ask God for... Perfection with so much gentleness, I haven't seen before... For nothing in the world would I have wanted to miss the opportunity to meet him and to deal so much with him" (*Letter* 12/05/1575).

◀ **BEAS DE SEGURA (Jaén).**

is a feast day in the village. The inhabitants, with their Sunday best, gather on the outskirts, next to the river, that in these first few months is quite full of water. There are drums, guitars and castanets. The young men, mounted on their Andalucian horses, show off their abilities before the young girls, who have carnations and orange blossoms in their hair.

When in one of the corners of the road, the convoy of carriages appears, the village greets the expected guests with shouts and cheers of joy. It is Mother Teresa, who arrives with her nuns to found a convent of Discalced nuns. The young girls sing verses and alleluias before the carriages that carry the foundresses; the young men mounted on their horses form a guard for them, and even the children jump and cry out around the conventual convoy, while the clacking of the castanets adds the classical joy to this particular Andulucian pilgrimage.

Mother Teresa smiles from the inside of the awning, thankful to such a friendly reception. She finds herself most welcome from the very moment she sets foot in Andalucía. And how pleasant is the stay in the beautiful Andalucian village for Mother! Three months of being treated most delicately and receiving gifts from those most splendid people, who see the presence of the holy reformer in the midst of their streets of white walls and beautiful windows of blooming geraniums and carnations, as a blessing from heaven.

THE PATIO OF THE CARMEL OF SEVILLE.

However, our saint doesn't want to make more foundations in those lands of light and flowers. But an order from Father Jerome Gracian, who meets with her there for the first time, changes her proposals and makes her set off to Seville.

*   *   *

It's the 18th of May. The sun burns on the Andalucian fields as it does in Castille. The carriages and some modest provisions of food and other goods are ready, and Mother leaves the town with six nuns, the chaplain and other assistants, heading towards Córdoba. First, they follow the banks of the River Guadalimar, looking for the shadow of the trees and the light water breeze. Then they follow the River Guadalquivir. The sand on the road seems to be burning and the covered carriages are like heated ovens. Inside, Mother Teresa and her nuns, well clothed with their thick woollen habits, are suffocated with the heat. And it is useless to look for relief. They don't find water in the fields, nor in the shops that are also reheated and full of rough and badly spoken people. Mother has a fever, has lost her appetite and feels ill. Her mouth feels totally dry, her head full of noises and pain, her body feels exhausted and weak... Not even at night time are they able to find rest, because the land conserves, as hot ashes, the suffocating heat of the day.

After three or four days of journey they arrive at Córdoba. It's the hour of sunrise on the festiv-

MOTHER MARY OF SAINT JOSEPH, THE FIRST PRIORESS OF SEVILLE.

ity of Pentecost. The city still sleeps in the drowsy atmosphere of the morning. On the outskirts, on the other side of the river, the bell of a chapel swings happily, announcing the pilgrimage festivities. Mother is quite happy to hear it, because in this way, they will be able to attend Mass without having to enter the city. The covered carriages that travel along the bank between the River Guadalquivir and the western walls of the city, are heading towards the bridge that they have to cross in order to get to the chapel.

But there are some guards who stop their way. No one is able to cross the bridge without the permission of the Chief Magistrate. Julian de Avila runs to ask him for it, while the carriages with the nuns inside await, next to the bridge. It takes some time to get the permission: one hour, two, three... The people start to crowd around the carriage awnings with curiosity, trying to see what there is inside. At last Julian de Avila arrives with the permission. He couldn't get it any quicker because the Chief Magistrate was still in bed when he got there. The guards open the gate and the travelling convent, with its back towards the city, well headed towards the bridge, starts to wheel slowly on.

A new impediment. The carriages are wider than the passage of the bridge and so they can't cross it. It will be necessary to saw what is protruding from the wagons. Julian de Avila and Gregory Nazianzen set themselves to work. The number of people that gather around keeps increasing. But neither Mother nor the nuns get down from the carriages nor do they lift the awning. In the end, when the axles have been sawed, they finally cross the stone bridge and go towards the chapel.

It is quite well into the day. The surroundings of the small chapel are full of festive people who have come from all around to celebrate Pentecost there, the patron of the chapel. When Mother and her nuns leave the carriages, the commotion is extraordinary. The figures of those nuns in their hemp sandals, with their rough habit, white cape and black veil over their faces, cause a tremendous stir among the Andalucian pilgrims. The nuns, mixed up in all the festivities of the happy and noisy people, are somewhat frightened. Mother tries to return to the carriages to continue the journey without having celebrated the Mass; but it is too late. And apart from that, Julian de Avila, who speaks with the authority of a theologian, assures that they are obliged to attend. And, guided by a good man, that defends them and opens a path between so many people, they finally manage to enter into the chapel.

When they leave, it is already midday. It is impossible to continue the journey now, with so much heat. The sun beams down like fire. The carriages and the roads are burning hot. And Mother still has her fever. It will be necessary to let the strong heat pass by. There, in a dry spot below the roman bridge, they find shadows, and a quiet breeze from the river. And they all refuge themselves there: nuns, clerics and muleteers, to await an evening not so suffocating which may permit them to continue their journey to Seville.

* * *

Whitewashed houses; small windows with grills filled with carnations; terraces that look like flourishing gardens; in the streets, rows of flowering orange trees. And above the roof tops and terraces, the silhouette of "Giralda", the elegant bell tower of the city's cathedral that stands out from the blue sky behind it as a continuous lookout over that flock of little white sheep that drink from the banks of the River Guadalquivir. This is how Seville appears before the eyes of Mother Teresa when, after four days of journey, she is able to distinguish it, at a distance, from the interior of the awned wagon.

But she isn't going to enjoy these charms of the Andalucian capital for very long. Having to live in a small humid and rickety house; without a bed to sleep in; with hardly any water; with difficulties, delays and mishaps that arise in the most unexpected moments against her foundational work, Mother gets so tired of it all, that she begins to consider returning to Castille with her nuns, without having inaugurated the Sevillian convent.

However, she doesn't do this. She ends up staying there one long year; one year solving difficul-

MISERICORDIAS DOMINI INETERNVM CANTABO

TERESA DE JESVS

ANNO SVÆ
TATIS
61
SALVTIS
1576

SAINT TERESA. The foundation of Seville conserves, among many other Teresian treasures, like the autograph of *The Interior Castle*, this portrait of the saint painted by Brother John of the Misery, in the year 1576, when she was 61 years of age.

ties, clearing up confusions, looking for help, negotiating a convenient house for the convent. In the end she achieves all that is necessary for the convent, and she finds a very elegant one: with an Andalucian courtyard, all white and clean; with a beautiful garden with lemon, almond and orange trees; with marvellous views of light and of colours.

On the day of the inauguration, Seville, so indifferent until then towards the saint, prepares itself for a great feast. The streets are decorated, there are groups of musicians and flamenco singers, long rows of people dressed with the clothes of their parish group, and religious that accompany the procession of the Blessed Sacrament. There are even fireworks and gun shots.

Mother Foundress is pleased with all that has been done. The convent is assured; her nuns are happy; the city attends to them; the authorities help them. They have religious and clerics who can guide them. Now she can return at ease to her homeland of Castille.

CHAPTER XII

HER LAST ADVENTURES

How good for Mother Teresa is the quiet time that she is living in Toledo, after returning from Andalucía! In a pleasant cell with joyful views over the River Tajo; without the disturbances of visits and business matters; with the loving care of her daughters; dedicated to prayer, to her writings and her sewing jobs, she feels rejuvenated in body and soul.

She writes at night time. One of the nuns, who observes her devoutly through a crack in the door, sees her seated at the table of her small cell, with paper and her feather nib pen in hand, writing incredibly quickly, what will be the book *The Interior Castle*. Sometimes she can see her enveloped in a gleaming brilliance which weakens the light coming from the candlestick. Other times, it is a lovely white dove that comes to rest on her left shoulder, as a beautiful image of the Holy Spirit

that inspires her. And what marvellous things she is leaving written on the yellow paper! The image of the castle of diamonds, with its rooms illuminated by the sun that shines in the centre; that of the fireplace where essences are burnt and perfume the room; that of the small fountain with its channels that overflow pure water; that of the silkworm, that weaves its cocoon to convert itself into a white butterfly... It's the spirit and imagination of the holy writer, full of light and fire which flow abundantly from the tip of her pen!

* * *

Meanwhile, in Castille and in Andalucía, the storm thrusts against her Reform. Her sons are being persecuted; her daughters are being calumniated and threatened; some want to finish with all that foundation work that had been built with so many prayers, sacrifices and tears. Now and again the thunder of the storm reaches her in her retreat in Toledo: the process against Father Gracián and the nuns in Seville; the subjection of the Discalced Reform to the "calced" Carmelites; the intentions and the attitude of the nuncio Sega, who calls her an unsettled and wandering feminine; terrible accusations made against the

THE INTERIOR CASTLE. This was the way in which a roup of young girls from a college in Madrid interpreted he Interior Castle of Saint Teresa with dolls.

most important Discalced friars before the Royal Court... At times it seems that it is almost inevitable that everything will be smashed to pieces.

In the most difficult part of the struggle, Mother returns to her first convent of Saint Joseph in Avila. From there she writes to the King, Phillip II, asking him for protection for her Reform. She doesn't tremble. Strong and firm, the saint explains to the great King the holiness of her sons; she discovers the terrible intrigues of their adversities and she assures him of the innocence of the Discalced Superiors. She also writes to the Royal Council, to the General of the Order, and to all her benefactors and friends. She trusts in God. But she knows that she must try everything she can to evade the collapse of her work. That is why she doesn't leave any stone unturned. She asks for advice, she encourages her daughters, she attends the Discalced Fathers, she avoids the dangers... And she wins.

One day the news that Phillip II wants to help the Reform reaches the grill of the parlour of Saint Joseph of Avila; that the determinations of the nuncio Sega against the Discalced have been nullified, and that a Brief from the Pope that decrees the autonomy of the Discalced, is on its

SAINT TERESA, PHILIP II AND LADYS OF THE COURT
An interpretation using dolls, by a college of young girls in Madrid.

way. Mother's eyes fill with tears of joy, and sparkle from behind the grill of the semi-darkness of the parlour. Her spirit rests, after the terrible insecurity she has gone through. The storm has passed. Her work has been saved. She can now return to the visitation of her frightened convents and continue her foundational journeys.

*   *   *

And the straight, dusty, endless roads of La Mancha and of Castille, after three years of enclosure, feel the footsteps of Mother Teresa once again. She travels through the provinces and towns of Valladolid, Salamanca, Toledo, Malagón, Villanueva de la Jara, Segovia, Palencia... The awned carriages, with their small bell and sand clock to keep the hours and regular observance as though they were in an ambulant convent, wheel on lazily, lifting up the dust in the summer time and sinking into the mud in winter time, carrying inside them, the sweet nuns with their white capes.

The city of Palencia vibrates with joy when it perceives the presence of the holy Reformer. Mother, is also happy, because she recognises there, the atmosphere of the primitive Church: purity of life, simplicity of faith, charity, patriarchal customs... Out of all her foundations it is where she was received most hospitably. Everybody helps her. There aren't any problems, discussions or difficulties. On the day of the inaugu-

36. MEDINA DEL CAMPO. The 2nd foundation (15/08/1567). It was here that Saint Teresa and Saint John of the Cross met for the first time. He decides to incorporate himself into the Teresian Reform. The actual convent occupies the same site as the primitive one and conserves part of it.

SANTA TERESA DE JESUS SYENDO NIÑA

37. **MALAGÓN. The 3rd foundation (11-04/1568). This interesting and beautiful painting is conserved in this convent. The painter imagined Saint Teresa like this: a child and dressed as a Carmelite.**

38. VALLADOLID. The 4th foundation (15/08/1568). Mrs. Mary of Mendoza, sister of Mons. Álvaro and Mr. Bernardino de Mendoza, took care of the Discalced nuns when they got sick in their first house in Río Olmos, and she proportioned them with a new one, where they are still living today, in exchange for the field that Mr. Bernardino, her brother, had given to them.

39. **DURUELO (28/11/1568).** The place was, and still is, so small that nobody could give directions to Saint Teresa to get there. And Saint Teresa got lost. The same solitude and the same scenery still surrounds this small and new convent of Discalced Carmelites in Duruelo, that calls to mind the primitive one inaugurated by Saint John of the Cross, the birthplace of the Teresian Reform in the friars.

40. **TOLEDO. The 5th foundation (14/05/1569).** Façade of the second house of the Discalced nuns in Toledo; the first one was abandoned one year after the foundation. This second house was a stopping place for the foundress in many occasions; and at its doors Saint John of the Cross called when he escaped from prison. Here, the saint wrote *The Foundations* and *The Interior Castle*, as well as a lot of letters in the most difficult times of the Reform.

41. **PASTRANA. The sixth foundation (23/06/1569).** The foundation of Pastrana was a whim of Mrs. Ana de Mendoza y de la Cerda, the Princess of Eboli. She entered as a nun in the convent that she herself had founded. The conflicts that arose between the Princess and the nuns were so difficult that the saint, in the end, had to withdraw her nuns from there (07/04/1574) and abolish the foundation. It lasted for five years and was the only one that Saint Teresa closed.

42. SALAMANCA. The seventh foundation. This portrait of Saint Teresa is of a very early date and is very valuable. It is conserved by the community of Salamanca. This community has been the most itinerant of all the Teresian foundations. The problem to find an appropriate house gave the foundress a lot of headaches, and she died without having been able to resolve it.

43. **SEGOVIA. The ninth foundation (19/03/1574).** The convent of the Discalced nuns was a few metres from the Cathedral and the church of Merced; proximities which caused more than one difficulty for the saint. She had this problem in several foundations of hers. The Discalced nuns are still living today in the same primitive building, even though it has been necessary to undergo several restorations.

Berdadero retrato de N.
U. P. F. Geronimo Gracian
De la Madre de Dios.

44. **BEAS DE SEGURA. The tenth foundation (24/02/1575).** In the foundation of Beas Saint Teresa and Father Gracián met for the first time.
Between the two of them there was a strong friendship and mutual
understanding which would last all her life. Teresa was sixty years of
age, Gracián thirty.

45. **SEVILLE. The eleventh foundation (29/05/1575).** Teresita de Ahumada with 10 years of age. In the first few days of August, 1575, the saint's brothers, Pedro and Lorenzo arrived at Seville, after having come from America after thirty five years of residency there. Lorenzo, a widower, came with his children Francisco, Lorenzo and Teresita. Teresita was nine years of age when she arrived and from that time, she lived with her aunt in the recently founded convent. Teresita was the joy of the saint and of her nuns in those difficult times in Seville, and she accompanied her until her death in Alba de Tormes.

46. CARAVACA. The twelfth foundation (01/01/1576). A panoramic view. In the foreground, the convent of Discalced nuns, where some cypresses can be seen. This foundation, as in that of Beas, had an added difficulty: both villages pertained to the jurisdiction of the Military Order of Saint James and it was necessary to have a special permission from Phillip II so that the convent would not be submitted under the commanders of the said Order (*Foundations* 27, 6).

47. **VILLANUEVA DE LA JARA.** The thirteenth foundation (21/02/1580). Catalina of Cardona, a penitent and odd woman, attracted the attention of the saint during this foundational journey and dedicated numerous pages of her history to this interesting foundation of Villanueva de la Jara.

48. **PALENCIA. The fourteenth foundation (29/12/1580). Mons. Álvaro de Mendoza**, as bishop of Avila, received and protected the first convent founded by Saint Teresa: Saint Joseph of Avila. He was named, later on, bishop of Palencia. In 1577, he invited the saint to found in his new dioceses. There are few people that Mother Teresa has written so many praises about as she has done with Mons. Álvaro de Mendoza.

49. **SORIA. The fifteenth foundation (14/06/1581).** "The foundress was called Mrs. Beatriz de Beamonte y Navarra, because she had come from the province of Navarra... She had in Soria a good, strong house, that was well furnished, and she told us that she would give it to us with all that would be necessary to found there... The bishop offered to give us a very good church" (*Foundations* 30, 3-4). The generosity, on behalf of the foundress, and on behalf of the bishop, Mons. Alonso Velázquez, helped to make the foundation of Soria the fastest and easiest of them all.

50. **BURGOS. The seventeenth foundation (19/04/1582).** Ana of
St. Bartholomew, the faithful and solicitous nurse of the saint, and
also the chronicler of several foundations, always took care of
Mother with a true filial tenderness. In this foundation of Burgos,
her care for her was more constant and necessary than ever, due to
the extreme weakness and illnesses of the saint. The foundress died
in her arms in Alba de Tormes.

ALBA DE TORMES:

The end of the journey. The saint, who was born in spring, dies during the first days of autumn, on the 4th of October, 1582.

Here is where the first journey finishes, the one that can be measured in years and kilometres: sixty seven years and thousands of kilometres. God's clock will now begin to count time from the beginning of a new and eternal journey...

51.   A general view.

ration, long lines of the faithful with their lighted torches accompany the nuns along the street, on the way to the new convent. Saint Teresa presides, with the Lord Bishop on her right and the canon Reinoso. Behind her are the nuns, between the secular and regular priests; the Government Council, with its Chief Magistrate and aldermen, and a great mass of people. While the clergy alternates with the nuns in the singing of psalms and antiphons, the musicians play their instruments, giving to the procession a moving solemnity.

Mother is joyful, she is grateful for the cordial and warm assistance of the people of Palencia, and because of some news that they have just told her that makes her heart jump for joy: the autonomy of her Reform. The Brief from Rome has finally arrived, which concedes juridical independence to the Discalced friars with regard to the Calced friars. Her sons will no longer be subject to those who persecuted them and tried to eliminate them. And there, below that clear and shining sky of May in Castille, in that city of so many charms of the primitive Church, the *Nunc dimittis* of the saint resounds, who sees her supreme desire made reality on earth. Her work is definitely consolidated. Now she feels free to die in peace.

* * *

With this holy joy in the soul, the distinguished reformer leaves Palencia. The countryside is full of sunlight and of harvest. The undulating and

A TYPICAL CORNER OF THE OLD PART OF MADRID.
Madrid was frequently a resting place for Saint Teresa in
her travels. Despite her desire to do so, she never came to
make a foundation here. In a letter to Teutonio de
Braganza she complains: "About Madrid, I don't know
what it is, but even though I am very aware of the convenience of having a foundation there for the other convents,
I am strangely resistant to the idea" (*Letter* 02/01/1575).

MRS. LEONOR DE MASCAREÑAS (portrait by Sánchez
Coello). She was the lady of the Empress and governess of
Philip II, the good friend of Mother Teresa, who donated a
house in Alcalá to be the convent for the Discalced nuns,
and in her own house in Madrid, Saint Teresa met her future portrait painter, Brother John of the Misery.

ripe wheat fields are lost, as in a sea, in the distance of an infinite horizon. Only the bare hill
with its high chapel on the crest, stands out on
that straight, monotonous view of the land of
fields. How deeply Mother breathes with so much
sunlight and such pure air, those latitudes open
to all winds and all possible dreams!

She is on her way to Soria. Besides the nuns
that will form part of the new convent, two
Carmelites accompany her: Father Doria and a
lay brother, two chaplains, a servant, a guard and
the young men who guide the carriages. It is a
delightful journey in spring time going through
very pleasant countryside. It's because they are
following the banks of the rivers Duero, Carrión
and Pisuerga, which are marked by two rows of
high and straight trees like giants that overlook
those great extensions of wheat fields and
ploughed land. The people of the villages who are
aware that Mother is going to pass by, come out
to bless her as a saint, asking her to make it rain
on their fields, prematurely tanned by the
drought of several months. First comes the rain,
and lateron, a miraculous harvest, left as a trail
of blessings of the sublime traveller.

They are now in Soria, the old city that conserves the memory of the heroic Numancia, its
neighbour. The Bishop assists the entrance of the
foundresses from the balcony of the palace, and
from there he blesses Mother, who, on her knees
within the carriage, with the curtains opened and
the veil over her face, receives the greeting of the

Prelate. Then comes the business matters of all the foundations: the signing of the documents, the preparation of the house that is to be the convent, the organisation of the services and the chaplaincies.

And straight away, she has to board the carriage again to travel along the roads of Castille; this time towards Avila, her natal city, going through Segovia, following the last foothills of the mountain range of Guadarrama, that she leaves on her left, so immense and green.

ALBA DE TORMES. The Church of the Annunciation. Façade.

CHAPTER XIII

A RESTING PLACE NEXT
TO THE RIVER TORMES

The Mother Foundress is tired. She has lived many episodes, gone through a lot of difficulties, and suffered many illnesses. Her spirit is still strong, but her body gives way. Her energy has been consumed, bit by bit, on the roads, the villages and cities of all Castille and Andalucía. And they are still calling for her and awaiting her in many places.

One morning, while the nuns of Saint Joseph of Avila are making the final preparations for Mother Teresa's journey to Burgos, the bell of the turn sounds nervously. A little while later, the voice of the nun at the turn is heard throughout the cloister, proclaiming joyfully: "Father John of the Cross! Father John of the Cross!" The holy Reformer is happily surprised to hear the name of the sweet Discalced friar. So many years have past since the last time they had seen each other,

and so many things have happened since then!...
Father John has been imprisoned in Toledo for
nine months; the Reform has suffered grave per-
secutions and it has been very close to disappear-
ing altogether. The two sublime reformers, one
in Castille and the other in Andalucía, have lived
some very bitter experiences, without hardly
being able to communicate with one another and
only by correspondence. Now, they finally see
each other after so many years, and after being
able to see the Discalced Reform established
definitively. They talk about all the things that
have happened to them, their mishaps, and hard-
ships. And they comment with enthusiasm how
the Reform has flourished so magnificently.

But Father John hasn't come only to see the
Mother Foundress. Before, they were living a lot
closer to each other, and he never gave himself that
consolation. He has come for her, to take her to
Andalucía, to the foundation they are to make in
Granada. He has all that is necessary for the journey: wagons, money and patents. Mother looks at
him with a melancholic smile. No longer can she
undertake such a long journey. Besides that,
Father John has arrived too late. The superior of
Castille has ordered her to make the foundation in
Burgos and they are all ready for the journey which
they will undertake the very next day. Father John
insists: the foundation of Burgos can wait. The cli-
mate is very harsh in that area at this time of year.
In January, it is much easier to travel to Andalucía.
A part from that, it will be the first foundation in

the province of Granada, and it would be most convenient that it be a job done directly by the Mother Foundress. The saint smiles melancholically once again, behind the grill of the parlour. It is impossible! She can't get out of the commitment to go to Burgos. But she gives all her blessings to the small house that will flourish below the shadow of the Arab Palace, La Alhambra.

They say goodbye. The black and profound eyes of Mother Teresa fix themselves tenderly on Father John; Father John's eyes look toward Mother with the expression of an eternal goodbye. It is a penetrating look, a deep one. They have the premonition that they will never see each other again in this world...

* * *

Burgos is flooded. The water from the River Arlanzón has spilled over the edges and it now invades everything, allowing the marvellous Cathedral to be reflected in the water.

It's night time. A group of nuns, friars and other travellers slosh through the water that covers the roads to enter the city gates. Sometimes they get suck in the mud; other times they slip with the wagons, that sink into the mud up to the axles. Father Gracián tries to give strength to the others; Mother Teresa smiles; the nuns scream terrified, they confess themselves as well as they can and pray the Creed, preparing themselves for a holy death. When they have crossed the pontoon

menester mas y v bien fundada
das sus obras y oracion y a saber q̃ la
primera piedra a de ser buena con
çiencia y con todas v̄ras fuerças li
braros an de pecados beniales y sigir
lo mas perfeto parecera q̃ esto qual
qier confesor lo sabe y es engaño
a mj me acaeçio tratar con dos con
sas de conçiencia q̃ avia oydo todo
el curso de teologia y me yço a todo
v̄o en cosas q̃ me deçian v era nada y
segun pretendia cuganar me v ste
uja pa ga sino q̃ no su poncos y tono
ti v̄ dos v tres sin este me acaeçio
este tener verdadera luz pa guar
dar la ley de dios con yerfecion
estuvo me ti v bien si bre esta sien
ta bien la oracion sin este cimiento
fuerte todo el edificio va falso si
no les dicen libertad pa confesarse

and they feel a lot safer, they all laugh, thinking about the danger they had escaped from and how scared they had been.

A few moments later, they arrive, soaked, at the house of Lady Catalina of Tolosa, and they have to sit next to the fire to dry themselves.

But this is not to be the only difficulty they are to find. The next day, Mother is surprised to find out that the Archbishop, who had given his permission for the foundation by word, bluntly refuses to admit it, and asks Father Gracián why they had come; that they can leave the city, going back along the road they came from. "And the roads and weather are so suitable for another trip now!" comments the saint when she hears this. And she stays there. Mother gets to work: she looks for help and some intermediary before the Archbishop; she speaks with the important people of the city; she sends messages to the Bishop of Palencia, her great friend Mons. Alvaro de Mendoza, so he may influence him in some way. In the end, after many trips up and down those muddy streets, many conversations and requests, jobs and documents, she finally manages to found the convent. It is the 19th of April of 1582. It will be her last foundation. The Holy Mother has finished her work on earth. She can now rest.

* * *

It is the rainy season in Castille. Along the road that goes from Medina del Campo to Alba de

Tormes, in the province of Salamanca, Mother Teresa travels with much fatigue, with fever, and without appetite. At one stage, she is so weak, she feels as though she is going to faint, and she turns to her nurse: "Daughter", she says with a feeble voice, "give me something to eat, if there is anything, I'm going to faint". They have hardly any food: only some dry figs, that Mother, with her swollen throat, can't swallow. This breaks the heart of the poor nurse and she cries when she can't assist the saint in anyway and she falls into her arms. "Don't cry, my daughter", Mother says to her, "this is what Our Lord wants now". And they continue the journey, wrapped up beneath the awning of the carriage that sinks into the potholes and leaks water, due to the rain that falls persistently.

On the sunset of the 20th of September, they arrive at the ducal village of Tormes. The nuns that come to receive her at the entrance of the convent are shocked to see her in such a bad state of health. "Help me Lord, as I'm so tired", she says as she embraces them and enters the cloister. And she has to lie down, exhausted with fatigue and illness.

*   *   *

The cell that the holy and sick Reformer occupies has the Tabernacle in front of it. From her poor bed (wooden boards with a mattress made of straw and rough blankets), she follows the prayer of the Divine Office with fervour. It reminds her of all the Tabernacles that she has put in place herself in her convents of Castille and Andalucía. And she thinks of her daughters, poor and holy, angels on earth, who live the ideal of her first convent, Saint Joseph of Avila. This is where she would like to die, and she says so to her nurse: "Daughter,

SAINT TERESA AND ANA OF ST. BARTHOLOMEW.

ALBA DE TORMES. In this convent Saint Teresa died on the 4th of October, 1582.

please do me a favour: as soon as you see that I am a little better, find me a common kind of carriage, lift me up and let's go to Avila". It is her desire, the last one of her life, but by a high disposition of heaven, she will not see it fulfilled.

The sickness is advancing. She has frequent collapses that leave her without speech, with alterations in the pulse and a brusque and irregular rhythm of the heart. They call the doctor; they give her medicines, they apply suction pads to extract blood. But Mother knows that all their efforts are useless. She is sure that she is going to die. "Daughter", she says to her nurse, "the hour of my death has come". And she asks for the Viaticum. It is the 3rd of October, three o'clock in the afternoon. The nuns, who surround the bed of their holy Mother as she prepares to die, are weeping. Mother looks lov-

THE DEATH OF SAINT TERESA. Painted by Victor Villán de Ara.

SEPULCHRE OF SAINT TERESA.

RELIQUARY WITH THE HEART OF SAINT TERESA.

ingly at them all. Petitions, sobs, and prayers are heard. And in this atmosphere of the small cell, with the smell of candles and premonition of eternity, the following words are heard as a last testament of Mother, who pronounces them full of emotion, and with a voice that is becoming weaker each moment: "My daughters, for love of God, I ask you to be very careful in observance of the Rule and the Constitutions, and be assured that if they are kept with the exactness with which they should be, no other miracle will be necessary to canonise you. Don't take any notice of the bad example that this bad nun has given, and forgive me". The nuns have put themselves on their knees, and the last words of Mother have produced an echo of sobs and tears.

Father Anthony of Jesus, who has absolved her and administrated the Viaticum, reads the recommendation of the soul. Ana of St. Bartholomew, her faithful and caring nurse, holds in her arms the head of the saint. The duchess of Alba fixes up the bed clothes and offers the medicines. The nurse recites with unction the verses of the *Miserere*: "Lord, you will not despise a contrite and humble heart... Create in me, oh God, a clean heart, and renew in my innermost a spirit of rectitude... Don't reject me from your sight, do not refuse me your Holy Spirit..." And then, looking towards heaven, with an accent of sweet hope, she exclaims, "At last, Lord, I am a daughter of the Church!" She will speak no more.

Sometimes she sweetly turns her eyes toward her daughters, who weep; and other times, she closes them and she recollects herself, becoming transfigured in prayer. Her face is becoming ever more smooth and shiny; the colour most gentle and transparent; the expression of her face, sweeter and beatified. She is in peace. Not one brusque movement, no contortion, no grimace. Three gentle sighs directed to the image of Christ that she holds in her hands; she lets her head fall sweetly into the arms of her nurse, and she expires...

It is the night of the 4th of October of 1582. The nuns perceive divine clarities, the fluttering of angels and the hymns of virgins, who carry the soul of their Mother. The smell of white lilies fills the small cell and runs throughout the cloister, perfuming the convent. On the roof, right above her cell, there is a shining light, and in the air there seems to be a movement of stars making the way for the spirit of the saint that goes up, towards glory. The water of the River Tormes, which passes close to the walls of the convent, makes a gentle murmur, as though it were to perpetuate that dream of Mother, who had fallen exhausted at its banks.

And it is there where her incorrupt body is kept, resting from so much travelling throughout the lands of Spain, that still conserves the small and perfumed footsteps of the great Teresa.

SAINT TERESA, DOCTOR OF THE CHURCH

(Rome, 27th of September, 1970)

After singing the Kyrie in the solemn concele-bration presided by His Holiness Paul VI , Mon-signor Pablo Puente, from the Secretary of State read in Spanish the following summary of the Apostolic Letters through which the title of "Doctor of the Universal Church" was granted to Saint Teresa of Jesus:

Teresa of Avila, the noble and illustrious virgin, reformer of the Order of the Blessed Virgin Mary of Mount Carmel, whose sanctity numerous saints have praised, and who many Doctors of the Sacred Sciences have followed as guide and teacher, has shone with her examples of life and excellence of doctrine in such a way, that she has been acclaimed uninterruptedly by the Church, not only due to the exceptional works of her life, but also for the brilliance of her Christian wisdom.

This has been the principal reason for which, in the same way in which Gregory XV conceded

Teresa the honour of the saints, the Supreme Pontiff Paul VI has judged it opportune to proclaim her Doctor of the Church, the first woman to be granted this title, taking into account her wisdom of the divine realities and the teaching that she offers in her writings. Already on the 15th of October of 1967, he manifested publicly his desire to inscribe her into the alb of the Doctors of the Church. This decision, based on personal contact with the doctrine of the Saint, is also founded on the high esteem that the Supreme Pontiffs, his predecessors have had of her singular doctrine, proclaiming this publicly on various occasions, so preparing the way towards a solemn declaration by the Church. Among them, it is necessary to remember in the first place Gregory XV, who asserted about the writings of Saint Teresa, that the faithful Christians could receive exceptionally valuable fruits of sanctity from reading them and the desire for eternal life. Pius XI judged as being very opportune and of great benefit the diffusion and the assiduous reading of the books of this great woman. Leo XIII asserted that her writings possessed a strength that was more divine than human. Saint Pius X called Saint Teresa of Jesus "illustrious teacher", Pius XII "sublime teacher of contemplation", Pius XII "singular teacher of sanctity and Christian ascesis", John XXIII "brilliant genius of the Church".

There is no cause, then, to be surprised to see that the very same people, so famous for their sanctity and doctrine, who dealt with Saint Teresa, never separated the praises of her sanctity from the excellence of her doctrine. These were the great saints Peter of Alcántara, Francis of Borja, John of the Cross, John of Ribera, John of Ávila. All of them considered Teresa as Teacher of teachers, inspired by God. Afterwards, other saints have shown the same esteem for her, among them we find Doctors of the Church such as Francis of Sales and Alphonsus of Liguori and others like Anthony Mary Claret, Charles of Sezze, Vincent Pallotti.

For all these reasons, His Holiness Paul VI, ardently desiring that the sanctity and doctrine of Teresa of Jesus be of great use to all, ordered that the Sacred Congregation of Rites study with the greatest diligence possible the convenience of granting the title of Doctor of the Church to women who, for their illustrious sanctity and doctrine, have contributed in a special way to the good of the faithful, according to the norms and decrees of Benedict XIV. The same Supreme Pontiff ratified and confirmed the affirmative answer of the said Congregation on the 21st of March of 1968.

Afterwards, before the petitions of the Superior General of the Order of the Discalced Carmelites, of numerous Cardinals of the Holy Roman Church, archbishops, bishops, religious men and women of all nations that postulated the proclamation of Saint Teresa as Doctor of the Church, all these requests were sent to the Sacred Congregation of Rites so that they be attentively examined. Lastly, the Supreme Pontiff, when he came to know the resolution of the cardinals of the Holy Roman Church, the members of the Sacred Congregation for the Causes of the Saints who had reunited for this purpose and had unanimously asserted that Saint Teresa was highly worthy to be inscribed among the Doctors of the Church, after having pondered with attention, approved and confirmed the sentence of the said Congregation on the 21st of July of 1969.

After having read this text, and after a few brief moments of prayer, the Supreme Pontiff Paul VI proclaimed Saint Teresa of Jesus Doctor of the Universal Church, with the following formula:

So, with sure knowledge, and after mature deliberation, in the plenitude of the apostolic authority, we proclaim Saint Teresa of Jesus, Virgin of Avila, Doctor of the Universal Church.

INDEX OF CHAPTERS

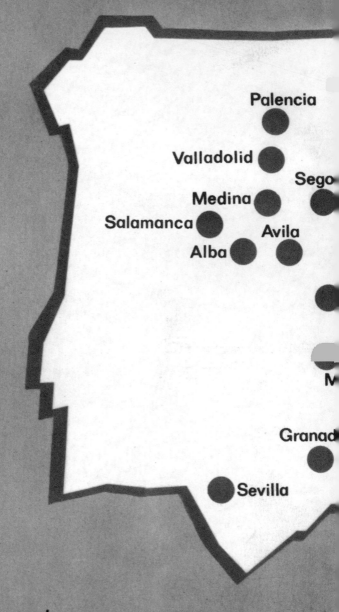

Palencia

Valladolid

Sego

Medina

Avila

Salamanca

Alba

Granad

Sevilla

M

1562/1582 FUNDAC

s

Soria

Pastrana

do

Villanueva
de la Jara

ón

Caravaca

Beas

NES TERESIANAS